DRU

SPORT

AND THE

YOUNG ADULT

Dr Conor O`Brien

ORIGINAL WRITING

ISBNS
Parent : 978-1-78237-154-0
epub: 978-1-78237-155-7
mobi: 978-1-78237-156-4
PDF: 978-1-78237-157-1

A cip catalogue for this book is available from the National Library.

Published by Original Writing Ltd., Dublin, 2013.
Printed by Clondalkin Group, Glasnevin, Dublin 11

*This book is dedicated to Leo and Eithne, and to the
teachers and parents who strive to guide our children
on a safe and worthwhile path.*

CONTENTS

FOREWORD BY RONNIE DELANEY

When my friend Dr. Conor O'Brien invited me to write a brief foreword for his book I readily accepted. We share many of the same values in relation to sport and fair play at all times. Our backgrounds include Olympic Sport. Conor has made a significant contribution in the field of sports medicine over the past few decades. More importantly he has been to the forefront in developing the Irish sports Council's Anti-Doping Programmes and served as a committee member on the World Anti-Doping Agency (WADA) for a number of years.

Illegal drug use, substance abuse and the indiscriminate use of sports nutritional food supplements to enhance sporting performance are contemporary and complex issues despoiling the pursuit of excellence in sport. School sports programmes are no exception. I am acutely aware of the timelines of the publication of *Drugs in Sport and the Young Adult*.

Nutritional food supplements are being used by young athletes and their coaches in the hope of improving their competitiveness with their peers. This is particularly true in terms of trying to stimulate / advance physical development as a by-product of an intensive training programme. The objective of the coach / athlete is to obtain the ultimate benefit out of the hard training involved. This is fine, many would argue, but a line must be drawn between what is legal and what is illegal, what is sporting and what is not. There must be awareness of the down the road risks to the health of the young athlete. Ignorance is not bliss and the coach and his / her athletes must be informed as well as parents, mentors and the school authorities.

The Irish sports Council is unambiguous in advising that there are risks associated with food supplement usage by young athletes and recommend against their use. Their reasoning is incorporated in a publication titled 'Supplements and Sports

Policy' available on the Institute of Sport website. Dr. O'Brien's book also lists the more common questions asked.

The use of nutritional food supplements within school sports programmes is not unusual. The Irish Sports Council and the World anti-doping Agency (WADA) are working in partnership on developing education programmes for under 18's to create awareness and understanding of the principles of anti-doping and managing the risks relating to the use of nutritional food supplements. The target audience however, is much wider and essentially includes parents, coaches, officials, mentors, with GPs, Team Doctors and physiotherapists and others.

The anti-doping programmes of the Irish Sports Council have been operational for over twelve years. They comply fully with the World anti-doping code and make a meaningful contribution to the worldwide fight against doping in sport. The aim is educating athletes, coaches, and other support personnel about prohibitive substances, anti-doping rule violation, control procedures, and the consequences of doping. Their programmes are exhaustively promoted. There is no shortage of information which is comprehensive and widely available on their websites and in promotional leaflets.

There are many questions posed in *Drugs, Sports and the Young Adult*. The comprehensive answers by Dr. O'Brien will, I am sure, help minimise the cases of young athletes inadvertently committing anti-doping rule violations and ill-advisedly using food supplements. The book is a strong endorsement of the importance of honesty and integrity in sport and the very guiding principles and spirit of sporting endeavour. I recommend that you read it if you want to learn more about sports participation and the well-being of the young athlete.

Ronnie Delaney
Olympic Gold Medallist

FAQ'S

- My teenager wants to take creatine, what should I do? (see page 103)

- Are protein supplements safe? (see page 114)

- My son buys cheap supplements off the internet, how can I guarantee they're not contaminated? (see page 114)

- My son/daughter drinks too much alcohol. What can I do to educate myself on its effects on his/her health? (see page 164)

- My son tells me he wants to "bulk up" and that all his friends are taking steroids, his rugby coach said they are safe to take. What should I do? (see page 116)

- My teenager is smoking Marijuana. What should I do? (see page 195)

- My teenager is indulging in cocaine. How can I learn what it's doing to him/her? (see page 185)

- My teenager smokes cigarettes. Is there any way I can get through to him/her, as to how dangerous they are? (see page 192)

- My son/daughter is very active but does not stay hydrated. What are the dangers of dehydration? (see page 175)

- I worry about my son/daughter's future because they deal with street drugs. (see page 181)

- My teenager is an athlete but thinks he/she will get away with cheating. What should I do? (see page 34)

- My teenager thinks it's ok to cheat. What do I say to him/her? (see page 60)

THE AUTHOR

Dr Conor O Brien is a physician practicing in Dublin. His interest in substance misuse in the athletic population goes back to the nineteen eighties when he wrote a Masters thesis on the topic of alcohol and the athlete. Dr O`Brien was the Leinster Rugby Team doctor and was Irish Olympic team doctor at the Centennial Games. He chaired the first Anti-Doping Committee of the Irish Sports Council, and served for six years. He subsequently served on the World Anti-Doping TUE Committee (WADA) and has also chaired the Anti Doping Committee of the Faculty of Sports and Exercise Medicine (RCSI & RCPI). He is a frequent TV and radio contributor to the debate on drugs in sport and substance abuse in society.

INTRODUCTION

Drug abuse among the teenage population is at an all time high. This practice is considered by many medical practitioners to be one of the greatest threats to the health and welfare of this next generation.

The pattern of substance abuse in society is now significant. Alcohol is used by over 30% of our teenagers, Ecstasy by 5-8%, Marijuana by 5-7% and Cocaine by 2%; while experimentation with anabolic steroids has been reported in 3% of female teenagers and 11% of male teenagers in North America. This book outlines the common usage and hazards of these substances.

Drug abuse is the scourge of modern sport and has infected it since the establishment of organized sport. Some of the first known instances of abuse date back three millennia. Detection of abuse only goes back thirty years; with formal detection programs starting at the 1968 Olympic Games.

Our understanding and knowledge of performance-enhancing drugs in society is at an all time high. Over a hundred years ago it was seen as a laudable, positive economic and health promoting practice. Today we realize that the abuse of performance-enhancing drugs is dangerous and significantly affects the morbidity and mortality of the abusers.

Like the internet, mobile phones, bottled water and doubled shot lattés, drug use and abuse is part and parcel of modern life. What two decades ago seemed far-fetched is now part of the fabric of life through which our children pass. Parents and teachers need to educate themselves in the symptoms and signs of performance-enhancing drug abuse. No longer is it enough to say "don't do it, because I tell you". Performance enhancing drug use is not a criminal act. Supply and trafficking is. An open measured, pragmatic approach to this form of drug abuse is needed, to ensure that young people are aware of the potential damage these agents can cause in the short and long term. This book is an effort to supply credible information to assist parents, teachers and users in understanding the risks and hazards of the increasing problem of performance enhancing drug abuse in modern society.

The information in this book is gleaned from lectures, articles and presentations given to both medical and non-medical audiences over the past 20 years.

An effort has been made to write this book in a readable format. There are frequent references to scientific research, but these papers are not referenced in the classical scientific format, to make the text accessible to the casual reader.

Chapter 1

HISTORY OF DRUGS IN SPORT

"The proper study of Mankind is Man"
Alexander Pope

There is a common misconception that drug abuse in sport is a modern phenomenon and that once upon a time sport was pure and an ethos of fair play prevailed. On the contrary: there is evidence of the use of substances that enhance performance dating back as far as 800 B.C. in Ancient Greece.

Ancient Greece

In 800 B.C., the Greeks had incorporated sport into their lifestyles to an extent that it was part and parcel of normal life and very much a part of the ancient Greek culture. Athletic festivals were common in the Greek calendar. Emphasis was placed on the artistic nature of athletics, as well as the role that athletic endeavour played in the preparation of warriors for the great wars.

Athletic celebrations at this time were also an important means of establishing the geographic, economic and political rapports of an area or a region. In the similar way to modern sporting prowess, Greek athletes were revered by their local area if they succeeded in athletic endeavours. As with modern sports, the successful champions were praised and showered with riches and goods, which left a profound effect on the young men of ancient Greece, many of whom greatly aspired to be as successful as the great athlete, Milo the Croton. Milo the Croton was considered to be the strongest man in the world during the 6th century BC. He was the most famous Olympian of his day. Reports of his exercise regimen described protein loading as part of his daily routine. Milo was several times Olympic champion over a 26 year period. He won the boys wrestling in the 60th Olympiad in 540 BC and was five-time wrestling champion from the 62nd to the 66th Olympiad, (532 to 516 BC). It is said that he even once carried to the Olympic stadium a four-year old bull on his shoulders which he slaughtered and devoured. He ate an average of ten to twelve steaks a day in his normal diet, in addition to many protein-rich eggs in an effort to maintain his renowned strength.

From 400 B.C., sport achieved a status in the life of the Greeks similar to the role it takes in today's society, where individuals align themselves with teams and support the cause. In ancient Greece, mass spectator sports were the order of the day. The combination of the affluent prizes for the winner and the social notoriety that accompanied champions led to the emergence of a class of highly paid sportspeople and athletes. This resulted in the demise of amateur competitors and the beginning of professional sport ensued. It was during this time that Galen, the much- vaunted physician, observed the use of mushrooms and berries by these competitors to enhance their performance.

Plato wrote that the value of a victory in the ancient Olympiad was the equivalent of nearly half a million dollars. This was complemented by other incentives which included food, houses, tax exemptions and even deferment from the armed services. Parallels can be drawn between the Greek athletic ideology and modern day ideologies in regards to professional athletics. Financial incentives drives today's athletes to be elite competitors. The only difference is the incentives today take the form of endorsements and sponsorship deals, as opposed to houses and food. Three millennia later, the inducements to succeed in sports form part of modern sport.

Professionalism and commercialism led to corruption in sport. Bribing and cheating were commonplace and competitors of the pre-Christian era were willing to ingest any preparation which might enhance their performance, including extracts of mushrooms and plant seeds. In addition to political interference, one of the significant reasons for the dissolution of the Ancient

Olympic Games was the use and abuse of performance-enhancing drugs which was considered by the authorities of the day as scandalous conduct that resulted in the corruption of young healthy men.

Early Christianity

The Roman period (approx 100 A.D.) confirmed that sport and athletes continued to have an elevated position in society. The Romans, however, adopted different sporting activities to those associated with the Greeks. Gladiatorial competitions and chariot races were the order of the day and these events served as a source of public entertainment, with vast throngs following the event. To accommodate the spectators, the Coliseum was restructured in 100 A.D. to hold 60,000 spectators. The use of drugs during this period has also been recorded. Chariot racers fed their horses a potent mixture to make them run faster while many gladiators were doped up to make their fights sufficiently vigorous and bloody for the avaricious spectators.

The Christian era marked a demise of these blood-letting sports. The nature of the dated Roman sports was unacceptable to the new order of society. In 396 A.D., the emperor Theodosius, called an end to the ancient games with a rule banning all forms of pagan sports. But while sports such as wrestling and boxing were initially promoted as substitutes for the unsavoury long activities, these were not widely accepted and their popularity as a form of sport subsided. It was also considered that the ethos of physical development hindered intellectual development and therefore sculpting and improving one's physical appearance were considered to be inappropriate. A healthy mind was considered to inhabit a healthy body rather than a physically strong body.

Eighteenth and Nineteenth Century

In the early nineteenth century, sport and professional sport re-emerged; this occurred mainly in England and quickly spread throughout the world. Societal sport in the early nineteenth century was comprised largely of unstructured recreational activities. England was agricultural and rural-based and activities were casual, communal and regional. They were associated with cultural and social events. Religious events or farming events would bring a village together for a form of entertainment and celebration and a typical celebration consisted of: Eating and drinking, dancing, sack races, leap frog, pig-chasing, cockfighting and boxing matches. Football games, in which there could be over a thousand individuals on the field at the same time, were also popular. It was in this environment that William Webb Ellis picked up a football to be kicked only into his hands and ran and thus the first few fledgling steps in the game known as Rugby Union Football began.

In the latter part of the nineteenth century, the rural nature of sport in society had given way to the changes that were brought about by the industrial revolution and urbanization. Many organised forms of sporting endeavour emerged. The reasons for the change in the traditions of sport were undoubtedly due to the wider change in society during this period, such as the Industrial Revolution which ensured people flocked to cities for work. Mechanical devices became more prominent based in central locations. One such device was "the spinning jenny" a multi-spool spinning wheel, invented in1764 by James Hargreaves.

The device reduced the amount of work needed to produce yarn. Advancing technology ensured that people move to urban areas for employment. There were many other mechanization developments during the 18th and 19th centuries which ensure further development in urban centers.

Communication
New forms of communication such as the telegraph, the penny post, newspaper and the telephone ensured that there was awareness about sporting endeavours taking place in other parts of Great Britain and indeed farther afield.

Transportation

Greater transportation ensured that the people could transport goods and services around the industrialised society. Improved methods of transportation allowed people to be able to travel more freely and indeed travel to participate in sporting endeavours.

Lifestyle

People moved to the cities for employment and the concept of broken time also became an important societal issue. Work time and broken time ensured that people had a distinction between work and leisure time. This leisure time was often taken up by sport or more pleasurable pursuits.

Political structure

The political structure aided in the lifestyle and also contributed to individuals developing themselves in the society. A middle class developed which was pivotal in developing a new society. This middle class had a particular interest in the new forms of sport and sporting culture.

During this period society was changing with female emancipation in England evolving during the end of the Victorian period. In the 1850's Elizabeth Blackwell became the first woman in the United States to qualify as a doctor. One decade later Elizabeth Garrett became Britain's first female medic. In 1894 Nettie Honeyball founded the British Ladies Football Club. In an interview to the Daily Sketch on February, 1895, she explained that the reasons why she established the football club: was to prove to the world that women are not the 'ornamental and useless' creatures , and she looked forward to a time when ladies would sit in Parliament and have a voice in the direction of affairs. Sports and society continued to evolve side by side during the late 1800's. A simple lack of space in urbanised areas also ensured restriction of participants; no longer could thousands of individuals participate in a game of football but specific numbers restricted to a certain time and space. Clubs and organised competitions were formed and rules were developed to instil boundaries and control in the sporting activities; as these activities were all modified, new sports such as rugby union, roller-skating and ten pin bowling evolved. Other rural pursuits such as cock-fighting and badger-baiting lost popularity and were eventually banned. The Industrial Revolution had a significant impact on all aspects of sport. Technology was used to develop new equipment, particularly in field sports such a golf, cricket and tennis. Two significant outcomes occurred in the form of increased involvement and interest in sports-commercialisation and professionalism.

As spectator sports were placed at communal festivals and religious celebrations, crowds travelled to see major sporting events and by the early nineteenth century, it was not unusual for a 100,000 individuals to attend a sporting event. This resulted in changes in stadiums. Sport was no longer a frivolous activity to be played in one's free time; sport for sport's sake was something that was the means and method of earning a living and moving oneself further up the ranks in society. During these years the drugs of misuse were in the main stimulants. Cocaine, strychnine and alcohol in different combinations were the concoctions of the day.

The German missionary, Dr. Albert Schweitzer made the first known report of the effects of cocaine use while working in Gabon. He noted that the people of the country toiled vigorously all day without feeling hungry, thirsty or tired and all the time exuded happiness and gaiety after eating coca leaves.

A participant in the endurance walking race in Britain, Abraham Wood, commented in 1807 that he had used opium to keep him awake for twenty-four hours while competing against Robert Barkley Allardyce in the endurance event.

In April 1877, walking races had stretched to five hundred miles and the following year, also at the Agricultural Hall in London, to 520 miles. At the time, the *Illustrated London News* stated: "It may be an advantage to know that a man can travel five hundred and twenty miles in a hundred and thirty-eight hours and manage to live through a week with such a small amount of rest. Though we fail to perceive that anyone could have possibly been placed in a position where his ability and this respect would be of any use to him and what is to be gained by constant repetition of the fact."

Spectators, however, enjoyed it and over 20,000 people came to watch the races. This encouraged the promoters to repeat the races at the same venues but on other occasions with bicycles. The *Illustrated London News* reported the bike races: "much more likely to endure the immeasurable publicity, a tired walker, after all, merely sits down, a tired cyclist falls off and possibly brings others crashing down as well, that is much more fun." The fascination with the six-day bicycle race spread across the Atlantic and the same race brought in the crowds, much in the same way that the gladiators of Ancient Rome did. More spectators paid at the gate and the higher the prizes could be, the greater the incentive would be for the riders to stay awake or be kept awake to ride greater distances. The exhaustion was countered by 'soigneurs', the French word for 'a carer'. These would be paralleled with the seconds in the boxing arena. Among the treatments which these assistants supplied was nitro-glycerine which was used to stimulate the heart and was considered to improve riders' breathing. Riders suffered hallucinations from the exhaustion and perhaps the drugs. Eventually public opinion turned against these public displays and particularly the psychological effect it had on the participants: "an athletic contest in which the participant goes queer in the head and strains their bodies until their faces become hideous from the tortures that rack them is not sport, it is brutal and it would appear from some of the reports that some of the bicycle riders had become temporarily insane during the six day bicycle races."

The first reports of drug abuse in modern sport came about in the 1860s. The first documented report was in the Amsterdam Canal race where stimulants, amphetamines and brandy were the combination used by the competitors. A similar concoction was used in 1872 in the New York six-day bike race.

The same year an American specialising in doping, Max M. Novich, wrote that the trainers of the old school used to supply treatments which had cocaine as their base. He declared with assurance that a rider (in the six day New York bike race) who was tiring on the sixth day of the race would get a second breath after absorbing these "mixtures".

Three years later on January 7th in 1876, Thomas Hicks an American was born in England, and came to fame in the Olympic Marathon of 1904. He crossed the line behind a fellow American runner Fred Lorz. Lorz's concept of marathon running extended to riding half the race by automobile.

Hicks himself who ultimately got the medal also had outside agencies to assist him in his efforts to win the race. He was trained by the famous coach at the time, Charlie Lucas. Lucas pulled out a hypodermic syringe (which had been invented in 1845 by Dublin surgeon Francis Rynd) and came to his aid as his runner started to struggle at twenty miles. Lucas is reported to have said, "I therefore decided to inject him with a milligram of Sulphate Strychnine and then made him drink a large glass brimming with brandy". Apparently Thomas Hicks set off again as best as he could. He needed a further injection at 24 miles to allow him to finish the race.

The effect this had on the runner was quite significant and he took many days to recover from the ordeal of running the marathon and only claimed his medal many days later.

At that time in the Olympiad of 1906 the use of strychnine was far from banned activity. It was considered by many of the scribes of the day to be a necessity for surviving the demands of such a race. The sports historian Alan Lunzenfichter stated it had to be appreciated that, at that time, the means of doping athletes for the purity of the competition had yet to enter the morals of sports administrators and athletes. After the marathon of 1904, the official report stated that the marathon had illustrated from a medical standpoint how drugs could be very useful to athletes in long distance races. The champion runner Hicks hung between life and death for many days but eventually collected his gold medal. He never took part in athletics again and suffered from ill-health for most of his life.

Almost at the same time, a professor of medicine in Edinburgh University who had an interest in mountain climbing was extoling the virtues of cocaine and the use of coca leaves for the improvement of endurance capacities in individuals who did mountain climbing. He identified in a group of his students the benefits to both the psychological well-being and the ergogenic aid of cocaine use when engaging in heavy aerobic activity. He reported his findings, in 1876 to the Royal College of Physicians. While there was much disquiet regarding his findings, he was not in any way banished by his colleagues but rather advised to conduct further research. This pattern of curiosity in association with the use and abuse of performance-enhancing agents has punctuated the history of drug use and misuse in sport, for example, the 1865 Amsterdam Canal Race first reported the use of medicine to improve athletic performance.

In 1876 Professor Christison reported in the *British Medical Journal* the physical benefits of coca leaves. He suggested that this drug (cocaine) could have a wide variety of benefits in reducing fatigue and improving productivity in workers, soldiers, the general population and athletes.

In 1894 Baron Pierre de Coubertin, a Parisian educator was responsible for the revival of the Olympic Games. He became one of the first advocates of physical education in France. His drive to restart the Olympics, after a 1,500 year suspension, was partly inspired by a visit to Greece, where excavators were uncovering the ancient Olympic site. De Coubertin was a romantic. He wrote in 1894 that "Greek heritage included training as a form of national defence, the search for physical beauty and health through a delicate balance between mind and body". He further wrote that "joie de vivre" existed nowhere else as intensely and as exquisitely as in exercising bodies. The Baron had formed his views on sport from observing the English public school system, where sports were an extension of education, and a means to "making men" with backbone and discipline. His views were based on an upper-class background where sportsmanship and the amateur ethics were central to the qualities of a gentleman. These ideal sportsmen would shun training, never mind drugs.

However the Baron's altruistic view did not penetrate all sportsmen. The financial and social improvement which was also available to those in the lower classes who succeeded in athletic pursuit ensured a culture of rule-bending. Evidence of this emerged at the 1904 Olympics, previously highlighted in Hick's use of strychnine during the 1904 marathon.

In the 1930s, amphetamines started to be produced by the pharmaceutical industry and were widely used by both German and Allied soldiers during the II World War. Steroid hormones were also used by the German soldiers; but the formulation was crude and had many nasty side-effects.

In 1957, Dr. John Ziegler observed Soviet Union weight lifters performing in the world games in Vienna. Ziegler observed extraordinary strength exemplified by the Soviet athletes. Following an evening of socialising with the soviets' doctor, he became more informed of the method of drug abuse that they had undergone. Ziegler himself had doped the soviet doctor who was quite intoxicated and informed him in detail of the specifics of the abuse of testosterone. Following this, Ziegler returned to North America and worked with Ciba Geigy to produce the first anabolic steroid which was a synthetically produced testosterone product. From this early start, anabolic steroids took hold and the world of modern sport was changed forever.

In 1952, a speed skater who was taking amphetamines and also competing in the Olympic Games, developed cardiac arrhythmia and retired from the games ill. While drugs appeared acceptable and supported in the 1952 Helsinki Olympics Games and to a lesser extent at the 1956 Melbourne Olympic Games, countries eventually began to speak out against the harmful effect drugs had on the individuals, in particular the individuals involved in sport and indeed the ethos of sport itself.

In 1960, at the Rome Olympic Games, amphetamine- taking Danish cyclist Knut Jensen collapsed, fractured his skull and died. As a result, the first significant anti-doping development occurred in 1960 where the Council of Europe, a group of twenty-one European nationals, countered a resolution against the use of doping substances in sport. The tide was beginning to turn from one of acceptance of doping to a more positive and proactive anti-doping outlook.

France enacted national anti-doping legislation in 1963, paving the way for Belgium to follow suit in 1965. The anti-doping problems until this time were relatively contained. It was not until the televised death of Tommy Simpson in the tour de France in 1967 that the International Olympic Committee became actively involved in international anti-doping initiatives. Tommy Simpson died live on television while participating in the Tour de France, when he was ascending Mount Venoux. He died of a combination of amphetamine and strychnine overdose. His death, which was observed by many tens of thousands of television viewers, prompted the International Olympic Committee to produce an anti-doping programme.

In 1968, the IOC issued a list of banned substances and tests began at the Mexico Olympics of 1968. A schedule of banned substances was developed, a schedule which is updated and unchanged every year by the current legislating body WADA.

1970-2010

In 1972, Dr. Bjorn Eckblom of Stockholm invented "blood packing". This involved removing blood from an athlete, the athlete's body then subsequently increased its own concentration of red blood cells by the normal stimulation of the bone marrow. In the laboratory, the removed blood was placed into a centrifuge where the concentrates of blood cells in the external blood was increased. This super blood was then reintroduced into the patient resulting in a high haemoglobin, high haematocrit-containing blood sample which could carry more significant amounts of oxygen.

In 1976, the East German ladies swimming team won the gold medal in eleven of thirteen Olympic events. Following the fall of the Berlin wall and the investigations of the Stazi doping policies of East Germany, it emerged that these individuals had been pumped with steroids and other growth promoting agents. The story of the East German Olympic swimmers is a sad one with one individual dying prematurely, one individual converting her sex from female to male having no other alternative and others suffering significant tragedies in their lives as a direct result of the drug abuse they were subjected to. It has also been reported that many of the women who delivered children in their twenties and thirties had generally passed on the damaging effects of drug abuse to the next generation because many of their children had birth defects such as clubbed feet.

In 1983, drug-testing strategies took an important step forward when analytical procedures were significantly refined. The introduction of gas spectrometry allowed accurate results to be continuously obtained. Also in 1983, the scandal of the Pan-

American Games occurred in Caracas where seventeen athletes tested positive for prohibited drugs and many others left the games without competing rather than being caught.

In 1987, erythropoietin emerged as a method of blood function enhancement. This blood booster was used for the treatment of patients with renal disease and AIDS victims, as it boosted red cell production. This, however, resulted in an increased viscosity of the blood. A number of deaths followed in young cyclists and orienteers in Holland and Scandinavian countries in the following eighteen months.

In 1988, at the Seoul Olympic Games, Ben Johnson the Canadian sprinter won the one hundred metres final in a record time, and subsequently tested positive for anabolic steroid abuse. These events brought drug abuse to a world wide audience, as a forensic media brought every twist and turn to a horrified , and unbelieving public gaze of a watching media and society. Drug abuse in sport became headline news for the first time in almost three millennia.

1990-2000
In 1991, twenty ex-East German swimming coaches admitted giving anabolic steroids to their former charges in the 1970s and 1980s East German swimming teams and were convicted of criminal acts. None of the offenders served prison sentences and some continue to train athletes.

In 1992, German pin-up sprinter Katrin Krabbe, Silke Moller and Grit Breuer submitted identical urine samples in early competition testing in South Africa. They escaped sanction on a technicality, but Krabbe's career was at an end. This case brought to light the cynical means professional athletes would use to avoid drug detection. Since she was the pin-up girl of German athletics, this significantly raised the temperature on the veil of secrecy that had involved the whole issue of drugs in sport.

In 1994, Diego Maradona, who had captained the successful Argentinean soccer World Cup team, was banned from the World Cup for taking a cocktail of five different drugs.

In 1996, Ireland's Michelle Smith won four Olympic gold medals for swimming. She was found guilty of manipulating her urine sample in 1998 and was banned for four years.

1998, the Faustina Team was expelled from the Tour de France and the trainer, Willie Voet, was caught with four hundred vials of performance-enhancing drugs. In the same year, Florence Griffith-Joyner (affectionately known as Flo-Jo) died at thirty-eight from a cardiac arrest. It was also reported that she had a brain tumour.

In 1998, Mark McGuire of the St. Louis Cardinal Baseball team made history by hitting his 62nd home run on that day. McGuire, who was a popular baseball player, finished the season with 70 home runs. His feat was widely celebrated and broke a previous longstanding record. At that time, many people believe that McGuire's achievements were tarnished by a revelation some weeks later that he had used androstenedione. This is a pro-drug (activated in the body) that boosts testosterone in the body and therefore boosts physical performance. This drug was promoted for its muscle build up and enabled him to perform these superhuman feats. McGuire admitted to taking it as part of his exercise regime. At that time, it was legal to buy androstenedione since it was considered to be a dietary supplement in North America although medical experts at the time stated that it was, in essence, similar to artificial testosterone in that it simply became activated in the body. While McGuire managed to escape detection because he had not specifically broken the laws of sport, the clock was ticking.

In 2010, in his efforts to continue his career as a baseball coach, McGuire came clean and admitted to the baseball public the fact that androstenedione was only one of many anabolic agents that he had abused during his sporting career; again the superhuman performance had in fact been superhuman and was induced by performance-enhancing agents. McGuire had given false evidence to the governmental investigations in North America and may ultimately face public sanction and penalty for his actions of misinforming the Senate Committee on drug abuse in sport.

In 1996, the Centennial Games at Atlanta raised questions about the effectiveness of the testing procedures. There were only two confirmed positive drug tests. For some observers, these low numbers confirmed that the athletes had become successful in circumventing drug testing. It was reported that some athletes hid contraband samples in their bodies and submitted these false urine samples at the time of testing. At this Olympic Games, there were concerns about the newly developed substances including human growth hormone and erythropoietin. The former works by increasing muscle mass and reducing body fat, the latter hormone increases the oxygen-carrying capacity of red blood cells.

In 1998, on the eve of the world swimming championship held in Australia, Yuan Yuan, a Chinese swimmer, was arrested at Sydney airport with thirteen vials of human growth hormone in her possession. She had been part of a very successful Chinese swimming team and the discovery of these agents confirmed the belief that the past successes of the Chinese swimming team may have, in fact, been drug-induced. This was the same year when the Tour de France travelled through Great Britain and Ireland. The event almost collapsed when numerous competitors, including top teams, were disqualified and concern about the systematic use and abuse of performance-enhancing drugs came to the fore.

In 1999, WADA was established as a result of the 1998 Tour de France scandal. It included representatives of the Olympic movement and governmental agencies.

In 1999, the Nandrolone (an anabolic steroid) controversy broke. British Sprinters, Linford Christy and W. Walker as well as well as Jake Hansrigger, Peter Korda and French footballers Vincent Guerin and Christopher Dugarry were all found to have abused this substance. This was the beginning of a long list of high-profile athletes who were found to have abused the steroid nandrolone. Nandrolone is a very long acting anabolic steroid. It was detected with the use of mass spectrometry which was introduced around the time of the 1996 Olympic Games. Adverse findings could be found much more easily by the use of mass spectrometry and as Nandrolone is a long acting anabolic steroid, it was easy to identify.

In 2000, Manfred Ewal, former president of the East German National Olympic Committee, went on trial in Berlin charged with 142 counts of being an accessory and causing bodily harm to the athletes under his change in the 1970s and 80s.

In 2001, positive findings of Nandrolone continued with soccer players Frank de Boer and Jaap Stam, who both tested positive for the steroid, in addition to Mandel Couto and Edgar Davids.

In 2002, British skier Alain Baxter lost his Olympic bronze slalom medal after he had used a Vicks inhaler and was found to have inadvertently inhaled stimulants.

In 2003, British sprinter Dwain Chambers tested positive for the new anabolic steroid, Tetrahydrogestrinone (THG). THG was produced by the BALCO laboratories in California. This was referred to by the athletes as the drug 'Clear' which was thought to be clear and undetectable. Many famous athletes who had abused this substance also followed a similar a pattern to the Nandrolone scandal.

In 2004, the Canadian-born British tennis player Greg Rusedski tested positive for nandrolone. It is considered that this drug was regularly abused among the tennis population.

In 2006 George Mitchell the U.S. congressman, who was instrumental in brokering a peace deal in Northern Ireland was asked by the American President to investigate the issue of drug abuse in the national sport of Baseball. He presented his conclusions in five sections as follows:

1. Major League Baseball's 2002 response to steroid use resulted in players switching from detectable steroids to undetectable human growth hormone.

2. Players who use performance enhancing substances are legally and ethically "wrong".

3. While players who use illegal substances are responsible for their actions, that responsibility is shared by the entire baseball community for failing to recognize the problem sooner.

4. An exhaustive investigation attempting to identify every player who has used illegal substances would not be beneficial.

5. Major League Baseball should adopt the recommendations of the report as a first step in eliminating the use of illegal substances.

In November 2009 Andre Agassi confirmed in his autobiography that he was a crystal meth amphetamine abuser. The day his book was launched to a world wide media; there were three near fatal cases of 'liquid meth' overdoses in Dublin city. There were no media press conferences for these three young men whose lives would be changed forever by their drug overdoses.

Agassi wrote in his best-selling tone "There is a moment of regret followed by vast sadness...then a tidal wave of euphoria... that sweeps away every negative thought in my head...I never felt such energy...I am seized by a desperate desire to clean." He went on to say the drug "makes you feel like superman dude". "I drove to Palm Springs played eighteen holes; drove home, made lunch...swam...didn't sleep for two days. Cleaned my house from top to bottom. Then sleep...of the dead and innocent."

Agassi was in the happy position to get help, write and financially benefit from his experiences. The three Dublin men and many of those who will read the vulgar and valiant claims of a drug abuser will not be so lucky.

Three millennia of abuse; forty years of detection

- 300BC- Galen reported the use of stimulants by Greek athletes
- 1865- Amsterdam canal race, 1st report in modern medicine
- 1872- New York 6-day bike race
- 1872- The American specialist in doping, Max M. Novich, wrote: "Trainers of the old school who supplied treatments which had cocaine as their base declared with assurance that a rider tired by a six-day race would get his second breath after absorbing these mixtures."
- Thomas J. Hicks, an American born in England on 7 January 1875 won the Olympic marathon in 1904. "I therefore decided to inject him with a milligram of sulphate of strychnine and to make him drink a large glass brimming with brandy."
- Strychnine at the Olympics 1904. The use of strychnine, far from being banned, was thought necessary to survive demanding races, says the sports historian Alain Lunzenfichter
- 1904- "The marathon has shown from a medical point of view how drugs can be very useful to athletes in long-distance races."
- 1955- Three leading cyclist nearly die on the Tour de France..... the second of June 1966, France's new anti-doping laws came into play
- 5,000 Franc fine and one year imprisonment, most riders boycotted the tour

- 1996- Michelle Smith wins four Olympic medals
- 1998- Michelle Smith banned
- 1999- Irish anti-doping programme
- 2003- THG and the Balco Scandal
- 2005- Two world athletic champions banned
- 2006- Marion Jones banned
- 2007- Baseball Mitchell report
- 2008- Floyd Landis Tour de France champion banned
- 2009- Andre Agassi admits drug abuse
- 2010- Performance-enhancing agent Clinbuterol found in three times Tour de France champion's urine sample
- 2011-Michele Scarponi, who won the 2011 edition of the Giro d'Italia after Alberto Contador was stripped of his title following a positive test for the banned drug clenbutrenol, was suspended from his team following his admission that he worked with the disgraced Dr Michele Ferrari
- 2012-Italian doctor Michele Ferrari was given a lifetime ban from working in professional sport in July 2012, after evidence suggested that he played a key role in the systematic doping programme employed by Lance Armstrong's US Postal and Discovery Channel teams between 1999 and 2005.
- 2012 –On the 10th of October, the United States Anti-Doping Agency released a report that laid out in detail how Lance Armstrong had organized a systematic doping program for himself and his team. Armstrong waived his right to contest the findings, 4 weeks later, the International Cycling Union stripped him of the Tour de France titles he won from 1999 to 2005.
- 2012- Italian jockey Frankie Dettori failed a drugs test when riding at Longchamp in France in September. He faced a hearing at the France Galop horse racing body in November 2012., and was subsequently banned for 6 months. His agents have stated that the substance was not "performance enhancing".
- January 2013 Lance Armstrong admits a life time of performance enhancing drug abuse.

Chapter 2
WHY DO ATHLETES CHEAT?

"Sickness is felt, but health not at all"
Proverb

Cheating in sport is as old as sport itself. Cheating is defined as an act of lying, deception, fraud, trickery, imposture, or imposition. Cheating characteristically is employed to create an unfair advantage, usually in one's own interest, and often at the expense of others. Cheating implies the breaking of rules. Examples include; Ben Johnson's disqualification for doping in the 1988 Summer Olympics or the admissions of steroid use by former professional baseball players, after they have retired, such as José Canseco and Ken Caminiti. Cheating refers to more than using illegal substances, and can occur insidiously and even unwittingly.

Athletic drug abuse is not simply a moral tale of bad 'poacher' athletes doping, up against good 'game keeper' anti-doping agents. The reason and rationale behind an athlete taking performance enhancing agents is multi-factorial. Its understanding may help to rid sport of this scourge.

If we return back to the beginning of the history of sports drug abuse, it is clear to see that the modern view of that day was that drug use in sport was a morally and physically beneficially practice. Galen reported the abuse of stimulants by Greek athletes in 350BC. In 1876 a Professor Christison of the Department of Medicine in Edinburgh reported in the British Medical Journal the beneficial effects of Coca leaves on hill walking and the potential role these leaves would play in relieving fatigue in workers, soldiers and athletes. This positive spin was also placed on performance enhancing drug use in the 1904 Olympic Games where the scribes of the day vaunted the use of Cocaine, Brandy and Strychnine by the Marathon champion. The pendulum swung the other way in the nineteen sixties when a number of deaths were reported due to the use of performance enhancing substances; Knud Enemark Jensen in 1960 and the notable the tragic death of the British cyclist Tommy Simpson on the Tour de France on the clime at Mont Ventoux stage. Athletes have always looked for a competitive edge. The reason they choose drugs is multi dimensional. Athletes and sports people abuse performance enhancing agents for several reasons. He or she may wish to:

- Build mass and strength of muscles and/or bones
- Increase delivery of oxygen to exercising tissues
- Mask pain
- Stimulate the body
- Hide use of other drugs
- Look attractive

There are a number of factors that may contribute to an athlete misusing drugs. These factors can be related to the drug itself, the person or their environment.

Drug:
- effects of the drug
- ease of availability
- legal status
- physical dependence

Person:
- dissatisfaction with performance and progress
- psychological dependence
- desire to cope with anxiety or stress
- desire to relax/socialise
- values - using drugs may not be considered a problem
- belief that others are using drugs
- temptation to think they can get away with it
- problem of being easily influenced by others
- lack of knowledge about side effects
- lack of confidence

Environment:
- friends or other athletes using drugs
- culture of the sport
- pressure to win from coach, parents, public, media
- financial reward
- prestige and fame
- advertising
- influence of role models
- unrealistic qualifying standards or performance expectations
- national pride

There are often specific pressures at play when a young athlete starts to abuse performance enhancing substances. If we take a seventeen year-old fifth year student for example; he is on the school Senior Cup rugby panel. He plays in the back row, and is enthusiastically training, hoping to make the starting fifteen for the upcoming Senior Cup competition. All his family has gone to this rugby playing school, and his uncle, who he admires greatly, won a cup medal thirty years earlier. His best friend who is taller has made the team. During Christmas training his coach praises his football capabilities; but laments his lack of weight. The young man is facing many varying pressures. How does he get bigger and stronger in time to make the team? His pressure points include:

- One's self
- The Coach
- Peer Group
- Family

One's Self
The basic desire to be successful and satisfy egotistic requirements is a major source of internal pressure. Problems such as self doubt, lack of confidence, nervousness, stress and depression are common to all athletes. The characteristics of self pressure are not exclusive to people in the sporting field. The young man in our example knows that performance enhancing drugs may

solve his problems in the short term; and provide a solution to the conundrum created by the coach's loose comments.

The Coach

A successful athlete is often associated with a successful coach. As a result, the coach may place direct pressure on an athlete to perform and may be the source of further internal pressure. In many schools the coaches are professional and paid for their services. Their remuneration is often based on results. Long gone are the educators who populated schools in the 60s and 70s; who gave freely of their time to train a team, seeing the participation in sports as an extension of the young persons education and overall development. In our example the coach has unwittingly or perhaps wittingly raised the issue of drug abuse. A road once travelled on may be impossible to get off.

Peer Group

Competitors set the standards to which an athlete must perform. If an athlete believes that a competitor has obtained some kind of advantage, then the pressure to also have or use this advantage is significant, for example; a better designed golf club, a lighter running shoe or the use of steroids. Similar peer group pressure may come from team mates. This pressure is frequently seen in clinical practice, where a young man often brought to see a physician by a worried parent, will argue the case "that if he stops taking his creatine, protein shakes, vitamin supplements or anabolic agents he might as well set up his running blocks ten metres behind everyone else....Give the other rugby team a ten point start...etc..." This peer pressure is based in urban myth. Every year there is a new magic bullet in the performance enhancing market, labelled a supplement, a vitamin or a mineral. It is said to be safe; and completely undetectable. For a price it can be purchased, but it's difficult to get large amounts of it. Frequently peers will connect it with a much admired sports star or successful opponent who is using it. The young man in this example is vulnerable and ripe for the picking.

The Family

The expectations of family and friends are often a source of pressure, particularly at the lower levels of competition. Similarly, successful family members may also create pressure. In this instance the young man may feel a huge pressure to make the team and be successful for the family. He may see himself as the family's standard bearer. Letting the family down may be a cross he does not wish to bear. Sports grounds all over the world are full of fathers living their own sporting aspirations again through their children. A famous American sports doctor commented that no horse ever ran themselves to destruction until a jockey was placed on its back. The jockey in this instance may be an overbearing parent or a coach whose actions and approach may provide the pressure on the young man to perform which may eventually result in him resorting to performance-enhancements.

Spectators & Crowd

Spectators create a great source of pressure both at the elite and lower levels of competition. At the elite level, athletes are often adopted as role models and will often take the hopes and aspirations of thousands of fans into competition.

Spectators are also the source of money and applause; hence the athlete may feel pressure to perform to standards expected by the public. The fickle nature of public support also creates pressure. Generally, we all love a winner and often adopt a 'win at all costs' mentality. The craving for the admiration of the spectators may be a temptation the young rugby player cannot deny. He might wrongly believe that "making the team" is his only way to "stand out from or stand up to the crowd."

Media

The media plays an important role in shaping the opinions and attitudes of the general public. How the media portrays an athlete, and how it reports on an athlete's performance. This can not only influence the public but the athlete as well. In a world where celebrities now hold so much interest and power, appearing in a televised school's match may provide significant local celebrity status; which may be very difficult to give up. The young man on the rugby panel has a lot to lose and, in his own mind, much to gain.

Social

Pressure for sporting success may also be the result of social incentives to achieve. The glory and recognition for sporting achievements is a strong motivator towards success. Sporting success may provide an athlete with greater access and mobility to other social groups, that is, successful athletes are usually given the opportunity to meet and mix with people outside their usual social group, such as members of the opposite sex, politicians and media personalities. In the case of the young man on the rugby panel the social aspects may not be his goal alone. Parents often desire the social attachments of following the school team; and being part of the 'special group'. The young man may be very aware of this and may feel he is letting Mum and Dad down, if they are not part of the new special social group. Hence the young man's temptation to cheat with drugs is multi-factorial.

Financial and material rewards

Financial and material rewards are major influential factors for athletes and sporting performance. Sport, which was once an activity to fill in leisure time, has now become a way to earn a living for some of the world's elite athletes. In recent times people have commented that money-making principles have begun to replace athletes' moral principles.

Enormous salaries, product endorsements and potential careers outside of the sporting field are some of the rewards available to the successful athlete. Rewards are also available to athletes at lower levels of competition and to those in amateur sport. Even at junior levels, inducements such as scholarships are a significant incentive, and can increase the pressure to achieve.

In the case of rugby a youth or junior contract may yield a young man a bank manager's salary. In times of economic difficulty bringing home a salary may be a significant pressure on a young sportsman. In the example at hand the young rugby player may be under an economical pressure to make the school cup team, and strive for a career in professional sport. This may be one of the only options open to him to achieve financial security for himself and his family. This was not a particular problem in amateur field sports in the past, as there was no opportunity to earn a normal living, but the advent of professional rugby for example, has changed this. Hence getting your foot on the first rung at school level is important. Failing to 'make the team' will make the next transition all the harder.

Sportsmen and sportswomen
Athletes by their very nature are risk takers. Anderson and McKeagh's research from 1989 showed that college athletes had a significantly higher proportion of "risky" lifestyle behaviour patterns; this included driving in motor cars while intoxicated, riding in cars as passengers with intoxicated drivers and a variety of other dangerous social and domestic activities. Hence the standard make up of a sportsman is to take risks. If an individual is happy to go down on a bouncing rugby ball with eight well-built men approaching at speed in an effort to wrestle the ball off him, he is not fearful of the consequences. Hence taking a risk of possible future health hazards with performance enhancing drugs is probably not a huge deterrent for the average sportsman. This mindset is often paramount in starting drug misuse.

Moral reasoning of young athletes
Doping; financial corruption; acts of violence; cheating and unsocial behaviour on and off the pitch are commonplace in the world of modern competitive sport. Research conducted by Shields and Bredemeier from 1995 resulted in "the game reasoning theory" which suggested that moral reasoning of young athletes is orientated towards personal gain. The justification of any amoral behaviour or transgressions of the

rules find their basis in the desire to win. Arnold showed in 1997 that amongst sports people the importance of winning needs no proof. Psychological research has also shown that in sport only individual interests are taken into account. This position is described as moral immaturity and seems only to influence the athlete in matters relating to sport. This reasoning is often fostered by their social environment through the coach's orders and peer influences. The team's bond and ideals are sacrosanct and cannot be broken. Justification of their position is often made by social comparison. "Everyone is taking the creatine, and the coach didn't say not to so it must be ok..."

Athletes will use moral reasoning to justify the sole desire to win. They will also use moral reasoning to justify misconduct, committing acts of violence and breaking rules of sport in the name of sport. In essence a certain behaviour pattern which is not acceptable in normal society may be accepted in the sporting context. Therefore sports people often use moral reasoning to justify their use of performance enhancing agent. It is important that coaches, mentors and school sports administrators create a positive moral environment for their young athletes, standing back from the 'win at all costs' mentality, and ensure that they the coaches are both moral as well as physical mentors and stimulate positive social behavior patterns among their charges.

All these factors - an athlete's desire to win, the desire to please the coach and family, the glory of victory and the social and economic reward of sporting success, often send the athlete in search of a competitive edge. Sometimes this search leads young sportsmen on to the road of drug abuse.

Athletes should be encouraged to learn self regulatory skills to help them ward off these pressures whether it comes from peers, coaches, family or financially interested parties. Failing to do so will leave them vulnerable to moral disengagement, through which they can justify the abuse of performance-enhancing drugs.

Chapter 3

DRUGS IN SPORT AND DEATH

"Whom the gods love dies young"
Menander

Drug abuse in sport has been known since ancient times, as noted in Chapter 1 with Galen noting the use of berries and stimulants among Gladiators. Sudden death in sport has also existed for centuries with the first marathon runner dying on arrival to his destination. 90% of those who use steroids also use other performance enhancing agents such as creatine, ephedra and growth hormone.

Many of these agents and combinations of these agents can have disastrous medical side effects. Drug abuse in society is very common and the use of performance enhancing drugs is no longer the sole territory of athletes; with many non athletes abusing these substances.

Therefore this problem is not just confined to the sporting community but to greater society. Every parent should be aware and have knowledge of this potential catastrophic temptation in their child's life. And it can affect the very young!

Competitive athletes have been the greatest abusers of performance-enhancing drugs with international pick-up rates of 1-2% in most national drug programs (ISC 2004) and rates of 20% reported anecdotally.

Most anti-doping programs concentrate on drug abuse detection in elite sport, with the important educational element taking a back seat. The core message is that drug abuse, be it performance enhancing or street drug use, is dangerous and potentially fatal.

There is a significant association between the abuse of performance-enhancing drugs and street drugs, with 20% of anabolic steroid abusers also using street drugs.

Cocaine abuse has been responsible for several well publicized sudden death events in professional athletes. Cocaine is often the street drug of choice among the performance-enhancing drug abuser. This drug has an added danger for the exercising athlete. Dr. Kloner in his article in 1992 in the medical journal Circulation notes the effects of acute and chronic cocaine use on the heart and its functionality. This is due to the acute sympathetic effect predisposing the individual to arrhythmia (abnormal heart rhythms) and by its association with myocarditis and myocardial fibrosis (injury and abnormality to the heart muscle).

In Ireland a 2009 survey confirmed significant drug problems in society with 2-5% of the urban population having experimented with cocaine, 17% have experimented with marijuana, 20% smoke and 89% drink alcohol.

The most commonly abused performance-enhancing drugs are anabolic steroids, stimulants, growth hormones, peptide hormones and masking agents. These agents are also potentially lethal.

Dr. John Zeigler was the American team physician to the 1956 World Games in Moscow. He saw the use of testosterone among the Russian athletes. He developed the first ever anabolic steroid "Dianabol". Some years later he stated "I have created a monster" which ultimately killed him and thousands of others. Zeigler like so many others died of the side effects that both long term and short term abuse of Anabolic steroids cause. He died of premature cardiac disease. Zeigler was not alone.

The cardiovascular risk of anabolic steroids is considerable. A number of case studies have linked anabolic steroid abuse with sudden death. A twelve year follow-up study of suspected anabolic steroid abusers identified a significant increase in sudden death with a mortality rate of 12.9% compared to 3.1% in the control group.

3,500 unexpected sudden deaths occur in England per annum in the 16-24 age groups. The majority are due to coronary artery disease. In 4.1% cases the coroner was unable to find a structural cardiac disease or significant drug exposure.

There are two fatal cardiac syndromes: Sudden Cardiac Death Syndrome and Sudden Arrhythmic Death Syndrome (SADS).These syndromes have no structural heart pathology but are considered by most authorities to be due to a rhythm disturbance in the heart's pace making system.

An Italian study from 2002 has shown clearly that all the commonly abused performance-enhancing drugs are associated with cardiac rhythm disturbances. These agents upset the normal working and function of the Sino-atrial node. This is the pace maker and generator of the rate and rhythm of the heart. Abnormalities can result in sudden heart abnormalities, which in many instances are fatal.

The world of sport is littered with athletes who have died due to drug abuse as chronicled in the following examples:

Lyle Martin Alzado, (1949 – 1992)
Lyle was one of the greatest American Football players of all time. He played for the Denver Broncos, Cleveland Browns and the LA Raiders. Lyle, a true defensive standout for the Broncos, was the first Yankton College (South Dakota) player ever drafted by the NFL and was a two-time all conference pick. From those modest beginnings, his combination of quickness and strength provided Lyle with the pass-rushing skills to start with the Broncos in 1971. His 4.75 second forty-yard dash time, coupled with his tremendous strength ranked Lyle as one of pro-football's top pass rushers.

His status as a premier defensive lineman was also enhanced by his versatility - he played both end and tackle in the front four with all-pro status. Lyle Alzado was forty-two when he died of brain cancer.

An American football SuperBowl hero with the Los Angeles Raiders, Alzado owned a restaurant in West Hollywood and had embarked on a career as a movie actor when he died in 1992 after going public. "I started taking anabolic steroids in 1969 and never stopped," he admitted during his pain-racked final days. "It was addicting, mentally addicting. Now I'm sick, and I'm scared. 90% of the athletes I know are on the stuff. We're not born to be 300lbs or jump 30ft. But all the time I was taking steroids, I knew they were making me play better. I became very violent on the field and off it. I did things only crazy people do. Once a guy sideswiped my car and I beat the hell out of him."

He described how his body disintegrated in his final year "Now look at me. My hair's gone, I wobble when I walk and have to hold on to someone for support, and I have trouble remembering things. My last wish? That no one else ever dies this way."

In 1991 before he died Alzado performed one more heroic act. He wrote an exclusive article in *Sports Illustrated Magazine*, the premier North American sports journal. In his article he blew the whistle on his own drug abuse and that of many of his fellow football players. The article was an effort to prevent others succumbing to the same form of drug abuse. His words are sad, informative and highlight how athletic drug abuse brought down the biggest of men.

"I lied. I lied to you. I lied to my family. I lied to a lot of people for a lot of years when I said I didn't use steroids. I started taking anabolic steroids in 1969, and I never stopped. Not when I retired from the NFL in 1985. Not ever. I couldn't, and then I made things worse by using human growth hormone, too. I had my mind set, and I did what I wanted to do. So many people tried to talk me out of what I was doing, and I wouldn't listen. And now I'm sick. I've got cancer: a brain lymphoma, and I'm in the fight of my life. Everyone knows me as a tough, tough guy. And I've never been afraid of anything. Not any human, not anything. Then I woke up in the hospital last March and they told me, "You have cancer." Cancer. I couldn't understand it. All I knew was that I was just so weak. I went through all those wars on the football field. I was so muscular. I was a giant. Now I'm sick. And I'm scared. It wasn't worth it. Sure, I played 15 years as a defensive end with the Denver Broncos, Cleveland Browns and Los Angeles Raiders and twice made All-Pro. But look at me now. I wobble when I walk and sometimes have to hold on to somebody. You have to give me time to answer questions, because I have trouble remembering things. I'm down to 215 pounds, 60 pounds less than I weighed just a few months ago, and I've got to grow back into my pants, they're so baggy. I've been in chemotherapy at the UCLA Medical Center and have done pretty well. I haven't thrown up or anything yet, but I don't have any hair and I wear a scarf on my head. The other day my wife, Kathy, and I drove into a gas station, and a guy there started making fun of my scarf. My "hat," he called it. I wanted to beat him up, but Kathy reminded me I wasn't strong enough. She said I'd have to wait until I get better.

I'm 42 years old. I have a nine-year-old son, Justin, who lives with his mother, Cindy, in New York. Kathy, who's a fashion model, and I were married last March, and we live in West Los Angeles. I got sick and went into the hospital two days after the wedding. And it was a few days later I found out I had cancer.

I know there's no written, documented proof that steroids and human growth hormone caused this cancer. But it's one of the reasons you have to look at. You have to. And I think that there are a lot of athletes in danger. So many of them have taken this same human growth hormone, and so many of them are on steroids. Almost everyone I know. They are so intent on being successful that they're not concerned with anything else. No matter what an athlete tells you, I don't care who, don't believe them if they tell you these substances aren't widely used. Ninety percent of the athletes I know are on the stuff. We're not born to be 280 or 300 pounds or jump 30 feet. Some people are born that way, but not many, and there are some 1,400 guys in the NFL.

When I was playing high school football in Cedarhurst, N.Y., I hadn't heard about steroid use by anybody. It wasn't until I got to college when I realized that, even though I'd been high school All-America, that wasn't enough to make it as a football player. I didn't have the size. I had the speed but not the size. I went to Kilgore College, a J.C. in Texas, and my speed enhanced my progress, but my size didn't. Then I went to Yankton College in South Dakota, the only school that would accept me. I realized I wasn't even big enough for a small school like that, so I started taking steroids. I don't remember now where I got them or how I even heard about them, but I know I started on Dianabol, about 50 milligrams a day.

The Dianabol was very easy to get, even in those days. Most athletes go to a gym for their steroids, and I think that's what I did. I remember a couple of weeks later someone mentioned how my biceps seemed to look bigger. I was so proud. I was lifting weights so much that the results were pretty immediate and dramatic. I went from 190 pounds to 220 by eating a lot, and then I went up to about 300 pounds from the steroids. People say that steroids can make you mean and moody, and my mood swings were incredible. That's what made me a football player, my moods on the field.

As I progressed, I changed steroids whenever I felt my body building a tolerance to what I was taking. It's hard to remember all the names now. I studied them a little. And I mixed combinations like a chemist. You had to take them both orally and inject them, mostly into your butt so no one would see the marks. I always gave myself injections at home in my bedroom. I got pretty good at it. I kept the steroids in my dresser.

My first year with the Broncos was 1971. I was like a maniac. I outran, outhit, "outanythinged" everybody, and I made the team after Pete Duranko got hurt in a pre-season game against the Chicago Bears. I took his place. All along I was taking steroids, and I saw that they made me play better and better. I kept on because I knew I had to keep getting more size. I became very violent on the field. Off it, too. I did things only crazy people do. Once in 1979 in Denver a guy side-swiped my car, and I chased him up and down hills through the neighborhoods. I did that a lot. I'd chase a guy, pull him out of his car, beat the hell out of him.

We had such a defense in Denver, especially that Super Bowl year, 1977. I can't say if anybody else on the Broncos was on the stuff, but because I was, I have to think some of the others were. But I wasn't liked on the team, so I really didn't know what was going on."

Lyle Alzado was buried in Riverview Cemetery, Portland, Oregon, USA. The coroner recorded his cause of death as brain cancer brought on by excessive steroid use.

Marco Pantani [1970-2004]

Thousands flocked to a funeral on the 18th of February 2004. It was the funeral of Italian cyclist Marco Pantani which took place in Cesenatico, the small town in which he was baptized thirty-four years earlier. Thousands of mourners gathered at the church of San Giacomo to pay their respects to the thirty-four year old cyclist.

He died from an accumulation of fluid in the brain and lungs. Investigators are looking into the possibility that he had been using cocaine as well as anti-depressants.

Many mourners who gathered outside the church wore yellow armbands to symbolize the Tour de France race leader's jersey. Pantani, who won the Tour de France in 1998, was nicknamed 'il Pirata' 'the pirate' for the colourful bandana he wore. He was a tremendously popular sportsman in Italy until his fall from grace in the 1999 Giro d'Italia, when he tested positive for performance-enhancing drug abuse.

Marco Pantini's body was found in a hotel suite in Rimini on a Saturday night. He had been at the centre of a series of legal probes into doping. Judicial sources said traces of what was believed to be cocaine were found in the room. Magistrates are looking into the possibility that the drug, mixed with prescribed antidepressants, could have caused his death. Italy's greatest cyclist had died alone, in his own vomit and excrement.

The bishop of Milan in his address stated that lessons should be learned from this senseless death. He reminded the congregation that "the man was mightier than the bike, and sport, and that no sporting victory was worth a man's life."

Marco's life on and off the bike was always punctuated with excitement and danger. He finished third in the 1994 and 1997 Tour de France before winning the premier event in 1998.

The 1998 event was marred by doping scandals. Willie Voet of the Festina team's motor car was stopped on its way to Calais where the tour was visiting. His car contained eighty-two vials of human growth hormone; sixty Hyperlipen tablets (to lower fat in the blood serum) and four ampoules of Synacthene used to increase the rate of secretion of cortisol from the adrenal glands. There were also two hundred and thirty-four vials of recombinant Erythropoietin. In short he was driving a mobile pharmacy containing potions and pills to strengthen the body and dull the mind. Sanctions and writs were flying around, the Festina team manager at the 2000 trial encapsulated the arrogance and disregard for the doping laws and their effect on the athletes when he simply stated in Groucho Marx speak "these are my principles; if you don't like them I have others."

Pantanti cycled through the mire to win in Paris. In the French capital, Jean-Marie Leblanc the tour director, formally thanked Marco the Pirate for saving the tour. Pantani's response was predictable. He stated "everyone longs for freedom. I'm a non-conformist and some are inspired by the way I express my freedom. I respond to the moment".

Within eighteen months Italian police had proof of Pantani's EPO and probable blood transfusion abuse during most of his career. In the 1999 Giro d'Italia he tested positive for performance enhancing drug abuse.

He spent the rest of his life trying in vain to clear his name, an impossible task. The last years of his life are described in the biography written by his manager as a constant battle to regain the lime light, and credibility, punctuated with the usage of a mixture of street drugs, outbursts against friends and loved ones, and with periods of remorse and depression.

He lost his fight in 2004, alone in a hotel room, drugged and hopeless. The highs and applause of the Tour de France a distant and unreal memory; he was now truly and finally free.

Chris Benoit

Wrestling star Chris Benoit killed his wife, son, and himself in gruesome crime spread out over a weekend in 2005 in the sleepy town of Fayetteville, Georgia.

Chris Benoit, born in Montreal, was a former world heavyweight champion, Intercontinental champion and held several tag-team titles. Pro-Wrestler Chris Benoit strangled his wife, suffocated his seven year-old son and placed a Bible next to their bodies before hanging himself with a weight-machine pulley.

Investigators found anabolic steroids in the house and concluded that the muscle man nicknamed the 'Canadian Crippler' was unhinged by the bodybuilding drugs which can cause paranoia, depression and explosive outbursts known as 'roid rage,' resulting in the murder of his family and his own suicide.

Authorities offered no motive for the killings and would not discuss Benoit's state of mind. No suicide note was found.

Anabolic steroids abuse has been linked to the deaths of several professional wrestlers in recent years:

Eddie Guerrero, one of Benoit's best friends, died in 2005 from heart failure linked to long-term steroid use. The father of Curt 'Mr. Perfect' Hennig blamed steroids and painkillers for Hennig's drug overdose death in 2003. Davey Boy Smith, the 'British Bulldog', died in 2002 from heart failure that a coroner said was probably caused by steroids.

'Roid Rage' is described as individuals on anabolic steroids acting out of the ordinary. Reasonable young men become unreasonable, aggressive and out of control. Autopsies revealed their brains had changed. The anterior hypothalamus, known to regulate aggression, pumped out more of a neurotransmitter called vasopressin.

Animal studies have show that young animals that are given steroids remain aggressive into adulthood, according to a study that offers yet another caution to teens who might try to bulk up artificially. According to the American National Institute on Drug Abuse, about half a million teens abuse anabolic-androgenic steroids. Other research has shown teen use can lead to psychiatric problems and heavier steroid use later in life.

Steroids increase instances of aggression by enhancing the activity of brain areas that induce aggression. Researchers have shown that this area of the brain is similar in rodents and humans. Some of the effects may wear off after withdrawal, but aggressive behavior won't stop immediately, leaving them to be a danger to themselves and others.

The Canadian Crusher had all the risks factors for 'Roid Rage'. His death was all the more grisly as the drug abuse ended the lives of other innocent loved ones. The successes of his wrestling career seemed to matter little at the funerals.

Steve Belcher (1980-2003)
On the 17th February 2003 Baltimore Orioles pitcher Steve
Belcher died. Belcher, who was only twenty-three when
he died, took diet pills containing ephedrine- the active
ingredient in ephedra, before a spring training workout.

The pitcher's body temperature shot up to 108 degrees,
resulting in heatstroke. While he also suffered from a
history of raised blood pressure, the medical examiner's
reports have indicated that ephedrine played a major part
in Belcher's death. Belcher's parents have since testified at
Congress to support the FDA's ban on ephedra.

In December 2003, the FDA announced its intent to publish
a rule banning the sale of ephedra-containing products.
The action was taken in order to notify the American public
of the unreasonable risk of ephedra's use. In a 2003 press
release regarding the announcement, Health and Human
Services Secretary Tommy Thompson stated that the action
was to be a sign to consumers "that the time to stop using
ephedra products is now".

Ephedra, also called Ma huang, is a naturally-occurring
botanical substance; its principle active ingredient is
ephedrine. When ephedrine is chemically synthesized, it is
regulated as a drug. Ephedra-containing products have been
extensively promoted in the last few years, particularly for
use as a weight-loss aid and to enhance athletic performance.

The concerns about ephedra are based on its stimulant-like
effect on the body which puts the heart at risk of adverse
effects. Studies by the RAND Corporation have found
little evidence for effectiveness other than for short-term
weight loss and suggested considerable safety and health
risks. Other studies have exhibited ephedra's use raises
blood pressure and puts otherwise undue stresses on the

circulatory system, which can be linked to serious adverse health effects such as strokes.

Whatever the research, another healthy young man with his life ahead of him died only because he dabbled in what he incorrectly thought were safe performance-enhancing drugs.

Dr Bruce Nadler

On Monday the 4th February 2008 the Los Angeles Police Department discovered former bodybuilding cosmetic surgeon Bruce Nadler, MD and his wife dead as the result of gunshot wounds. Authorities believe it was an apparent murder/suicide perpetrated by Bruce Nadler.

Bruce Nadler called himself the "world's strongest plastic surgeon." He was probably the best known cosmetic surgeon catering to amateur and professional bodybuilders. He had performed over seven hundred gynecomastia surgeries in his career; 'gyno' a slang word used by bodybuilders, is a side effect of anabolic steroid use when antiaromatase and/or estrogen antagonists are not use concurrently, resulting in abnormal breast tissue growth.

After retiring from the practice of medicine in August 2005, Dr. Nadler, wrote the 'The Nip Tuck Workout: Exercise through the Eyes of a Plastic Surgeon'. He subsequently moved with his wife to Los Angeles to reinvent himself in a new career as personal trainer with the opening of Nip Tuck Fitness LA *in Beverly Hills. His death and the death of his wife were considered to be due to the chronic psychological effects of anabolic steroid abuse, known as 'Roid Rage'.*

Terry Newton (1979-2010)

On the 28th September 2010 the Great British rugby league star Terry Newton was found hanged at his home, seven months after he was suspended from the game for two years. He was found guilty of taking the banned human growth hormone drug. Police said there were no suspicious circumstances, and suicide was suspected.

Terry posted an apparent suicide note on his Facebook page in the early hours before his death. It read: "Luv u all but end time xxxx". Newton lost his contract with Wakefield Rugby League Club due to the drug scandal. After his suspension he bought a pub with his father-in-law and started a new career as a landlord.

He was married with two children and had suffered from depression in the past, sparked by the death of his younger sister from heroin abuse in 2008. Two-times Challenge Cup winner Newton's body was found at his home in Orrell near Wigan. In a TV interview three weeks before his death, he admitted he wanted to play again. Newton said: "Every day I wish I was going to training with the lads. I miss the craic."

The star, who also grew up in Wigan, began experimenting with Human Growth Hormone in July 2009 while injured. He was so impressed by how it speeded up recovery that he carried on injecting it. He was thirty-one when he died.

Chapter 4

DRUG ABUSE IN SPORT AND THE ASSOCIATION WITH CRIMINALITY AND CRIMINAL ACTS

"Cain was a juvenile delinquent without being born on the wrong side of the tracks"
Anon

The world of performance-enhancing drug abuse can act as a gateway to other significant social problems for the innocent drug abuser. The majority of performance-enhancing drugs are sold illegally as contraband. Hence an abuser enters the world of suppliers and criminality to obtain his fix. Once he has entered this world other temptations and options become available, and the association with criminality and criminal acts is strong. The British crime surveys of 1996 and 2000 stated that performance enhancing drug abuse was "A society problem not just sports issue." The 1996 survey highlighted the facts that 1% of male and 1% of female arrestees between the ages of sixteen and fifty-nine had used Anabolic Steroids. The highest abusing group was the twenty to twenty-four year-old males (making up 3% of the arrestees).

The 2000 survey showed that 1% of all arrestees had used anabolic steroids in the previous year. Of the seventeen to twenty-five year-olds who were arrested a staggering 5% had taken these performance-enhancing agents.

These surveys show that performance-enhancing drug abuse is a societal problem. The use of these agents puts the young adult 'in the way' of trouble. He or she tends to mix with unscrupulous individuals who populate the world of drug trafficking (both performance and street drugs). They often

DRUGS, SPORT AND THE YOUNG ADULT

find themselves in compromising situations but will tend to conform and go with the herd mentality. They often become part of the group and as the abuse is shrouded in secrecy it can be difficult to disengage easily. They too can then become dealers and experts in the area of performance enhancing drug abuse.

Vulnerable abusers are often groomed to be sellers and dealers; the grooming taking place away from their normal domestic and school setting.

The social market for these agents is also huge and performance-enhancing drug abuse is rife among social sets that frequent the 'midnight hours'. Boys look fitter and stronger, and girls are leaner on these substances; hence they are often available in night clubs and bars as an addition to street drugs. The association of the abuse of both agents is strong: there is a significant association between the abuse of performance-enhancing drugs and street drugs, with 20% of anabolic steroid abusers also using street drugs.

Hence involvement in the world of drug abuse in sport can have devastating social consequences. Here are a number of examples of how life changed dramatically for certain individuals, who became involved in the murky world of performance enhancing drug abuse.

Victor Conte

Victor Conte was the founder of BALCO- Bay Area Laboratory Cooperative. A former bass player with soul group Tower of Power and jazz pianist Herbie Hancock, he founded BALCO in the early nineteen-eighties.

The company BALCO analyses blood and urine from athletes and then prescribes a series of supplements to compensate for vitamin and mineral deficiencies.

Among its clients were top athletes Marion Jones and Tim Montgomery, as well as baseball star Barry Bonds and the NFL's Bill Romanowski.

Bonds had been a BALCO client since the winter of 2000 and had credited the company for a personalised programme that included nutritional supplements.

BALCO has been identified by the United States Anti-Doping Agency (USADA) as the source of the anabolic steroid THG, know by the slang name of 'Clear'. BALCO groups advised their clients that the drug was undetectable by conventional drug testing methods. The world changed for the drug cheats when a whistle blower entered the fray. The USADA was contacted by an anonymous athletics coach who claimed that several top athletes were using THG.

The same coach then handed over a syringe containing THG, which USADA used to develop an effective test for the substance. Urine samples taken at the U.S. championships were then re-tested, resulting in a number of positive tests. The apparently 'clear drug' became quite opaque; many sporting careers were unmasked as a sham. What followed for the drug abusers and drug peddlers was misery and prison time.

On 1st December 2005 Victor Conte began a four-month prison sentence; a further four months home confinement for drugs offences followed. Conte, fifty-four, was also given two years of court supervision for his role in a scheme to give athletes undetectable performance-enhancing drugs. Baseball star Barry Bonds' trainer, Greg Anderson, was convicted of money laundering and steroid distribution. The childhood friend of Bonds spent three months in home confinement.

BALCO vice-president James Valente was placed on probation after pleading guilty to reduced charges of steroid distribution. The BALCO scandal has involved some of athletics' top names, with Dwain Chambers and former world double sprint champion Kelli White both receiving two-year bans.

The plea-bargain sentences have been criticised by some anti-doping officials as too lenient.

Marion Jones
American Olympian Marion Jones was sentenced to six months in prison for lying about steroid use and involvement in a drugs fraud case. The former sprinter pleaded guilty, admitting to using a steroid between September 2000 and July 2001. The mother-of-two aged thirty-two at the time, had asked U.S. district judge Kenneth Karas to be "as merciful as a human being can be". Jones told the judge she was "deeply sorry" and asked the judge to consider her commitment to her two children, including an infant son she was nursing. "Your honor, I absolutely realize the gravity of these offences and I am deeply sorry," she said.

But the judge imposed the maximum under her plea deal "because of the need for general deterrence and the need to promote respect for the law". Lawyers for the prosecution had suggested any sentence between probation and six months would be fair. He said he believed a message needed to be sent to athletes who have abused drugs and as a result, have overlooked the values of "hard work, dedication, teamwork and sportsmanship"... Athletes in society have an elevated status, they entertain, they inspire, and perhaps, most important, they serve as role models." He added "Nobody is above the legal obligation to tell the truth."

Jones also pleaded guilty to lying to federal investigators in 2003 about a separate cheque fraud case involving her former boyfriend, sprinter Tim Montgomery, the father of her son, Monty.

Judge Karas had sought advice as to whether he could go beyond the six-month maximum sentence suggested in the plea deal. "The offences here are serious. They each involve lies made three years apart," he said, adding that Jones had made "not a one-off mistake... but a repetition in an attempt to break the law". He said he did not believe a statement by Jones in October when she said she did not realize she was taking steroids until after the 2000 Olympic Games. "That is very difficult to believe, that a top-notch athlete... would not be keenly aware of what he or she put in her body," the judge said.

Afterwards Jones said outside court: "I respect the judge's order, and I truly hope that people will learn from my mistakes."

Lawyers for the defense had asked the judge to give the former sprinter probation or house arrest. Having already apologized, retired and given up her five Olympic medals, Jones has been punished enough, they argued. Jones sentencing included two years' probation and supervised release, during which she was required to perform eight hundred hours of community service.

Once arguably the most famous female athlete in the world, Jones won gold in the 100m, 200m and 4 x 100m relay as well as bronze in the long jump and 4x100m relay, at the Sydney Olympics in 2000.

While her charisma and big smile won her a global fan base, her success on the track coupled with photogenic looks won her lucrative endorsements. But she suffered a spectacular fall from glory after admitting lying to a federal investigator in November 2003 when she denied using performance-enhancing drugs.

Jones, who returned her medals even before the International Olympic Committee ordered her to do so, has since had her name expunged from the record books. Hers was one of a number of high-profile doping cases involving top American athletes that have prompted the U.S. Olympic Committee to team up with Major League Baseball and the National Football League with a new initiative aimed at combating drug use in U.S. sport.

Floyd Landis

In 2006, Landis won the first edition of the Tour of California, before going on to finish first in the 2006 Tour de France. He was stripped of his Tour de France victory and fired from the Phonak team after a drug-control test demonstrated the presence of a skewed testosterone/ epitestosterone ratio during stage seventeen. The ratio was 1:6.

Most people have a ration of testosterone to epitestosterone of 1:1. This is known as the T/E ratio. Epitestosterone is the precursor to testosterone in normal metabolism. In simple terms for every unit of testosterone produced there should be a similar unit of the precursor. If exogenous testosterone, or an anabolic steroid is taken by an individual, the testosterone level will rise, but there will be no change in the epitestosterone level. Hence the ratio will skew. This ratio is the basis of one of the tests on which anti-doping agencies access for anabolic steroid abuse. In rare metabolic situations this ratio can be altered naturally, and this in unusual cases may rise to 1: 3. These cases are exceptional. Nevertheless the doping authorities have taken this rarity into account and allow a ratio of up to 1: 4. This test assesses the T/E ratio in the urine. Landis sample showed a significantly altered T/E ratio of 1:6.

On 20th September 2007, Floyd Landis was stripped of his title as winner of the Tour de France, and was subjected to a two year ban from professional racing after a second test showing an elevated T/E ratio. Landis won the seventeenth stage of the tour; however, tests taken immediately after the stage victory showed a T/E ratio of 11:1, more than double the 4:1 imposed limit. This ratio limit has been lowered from previous limits of 8:1 and 6:1.

On 1st August 2006, media reports said that synthetic testosterone had been detected in the A sample, using the carbon isotope ratio test (CIR). The presence of synthetic testosterone means that some of the testosterone in Landis's body came from an external source and was not naturally produced by his own system. These results conflict with Landis's public speculation that it was a natural occurrence. Landis had emphatically denied the charge; pointing out the scientific data that testosterone cannot enhance athletic performance unless taken over an extended period of time with regular doses.

Landis maintained his innocence, and he mounted a vigorous defense. Although Landis's legal team documented inconsistencies in the handling and evaluation of his urine samples, the disqualification was upheld.

He was suspended from professional competition until 30th of January 2009, following an arbitration panel's two to one ruling on the twentieth of September 2007. Landis appealed the result of the arbitration hearing to the Court of Arbitration for Sport, which subsequently upheld the panel's ruling.

Landis attempted to return to cycling in 2009 ,but his performances were poor. In 2010 he "about turned" in his position of innocence, when he admitted publically his long drug abuse, and that of many other fellow cyclists. His abuse was initially detected in a urine sample showing an abnormal T/E ratio.

The ratio of the concentration of testosterone to the concentration of epitestosterone (T/E ratio) as determined in urine is the most frequently used method to prove testosterone abuse by athletes. A T/E ratio higher than six has been considered as proof of abuse in the past; however, cases of naturally occurring higher T/E ratios have been described. Since the introduction of the T/E ratio in doping analysis, the parameters that may or may not increase the T/E ratio, possibly leading to false-positive results, have been debated.

In 1996 the U.S. athlete Mary Decker failed a T/E test with a T/E ratio of greater than six, the limit in force at the time. She took the case to arbitration, arguing that birth control pills can cause false positives for the test, but the arbitration panel ruled against her.

American cyclist Floyd Landis was wanted by French authorities in connection to a hacking incident at a national anti-doping laboratory. The rider denied any involvement in the case. Landis told the Los Angeles Times that he was formally contacted regarding the recent developments and stated that the arrest warrant only covered France. What a long way from the adulation of the podium and the Yellow Jersey.

Performance-enhancing drug abuse is both directly and indirectly associated with criminality. Parents of children embarking on this practice need to be aware of the lifestyle and potential social consequences of this activity. The law enforcement authorities have their eyes peeled on the road of drug production and supply, to the use, misuse and avoidance of detection. Entering this world, even with good intentions, can lead to a criminal record and social destruction.

Chapter 5

PERFORMANCE ENHANCING DRUGS
AND BODY IMAGE

"Beauty in form and feature, Lovely as the day,
Can there be so fair a creature, Formed of common clay"
Henry W Longfellow

The history of female and male body image dates back to the dawn of mankind. However, female beauty and the need to achieve a standard of beauty or physical perfection have changed continually throughout the history of mankind.

In ancient Egypt, women and men strove to attain a godlike physique and persona. The ancient Greeks and Romans did the same, though their gods were different.

The western world is awash with images of sexy, impossibly perfect bodies, and this bombardment of images of physical perfection is greatly affecting our perception of our own physicality. Some people are convinced that they are horribly ugly or deformed, even when they look perfectly normal. This is sometimes referred to as Body Dysmorphic Disorder (BBD). Up to 2.4% of the population may suffer from this condition.

People with BDD are often so fearful of being seen outside of a controlled setting owing to their skewed sense of self that they avoid any social situation, be it meetings, parties, or other gatherings.

Although it is often thought to be a problem that affects mainly women, BDD affects men too. In fact, about 40% of BDD sufferers are male, and the disorder is significantly more common than many realize. Individuals who suffer from BDD frequently spend numerous hours a day physically working out and become consumed with their physical image; resulting in both physical and mental issues.

Men who suffer from a form of BDD known as muscle dysphoria, or 'bigorexia,' often become compulsive weight-lifters. These individuals frequently turn to anabolic steroids in a misguided attempt to bulk up. Research suggests that the disorder may materialize from emotional factors - for example, being teased a lot during childhood.

The constant hammering of the consciousness of images of impossibly muscular and thin men and women can leave the susceptible individual vulnerable and believing in the ability to attain the statuesque bodies that are presented in these air-brushed photographs and other forms of media.

In the early part of the twentieth century, women were struggling for independence from the constraints of the Victorian era. The classical standard of beauty was still very much thriving and people strove to attain a traditional fair skinned and well-rounded figure. In those days, a full figure was a good thing and the Gibson Girl personified this classical image of womanhood.

With the right to vote came freedom and independence for many women. For the first time in United States history, women had a voice and the ability to freely express themselves as they chose. Many women chose to dress as 'flappers' and wore the characteristic short skirts and dresses that flaunted their assets to the world. The flapper style waved goodbye to long hair and concealed appendages, and said hello to long legs and a somewhat androgynous bob hairstyle.

By the nineteen thirties, the film industry had begun to produce the first movie stars and some might call it the 'age of glamour'. Clothes were still tailor-made and popular fabrics of the day such as silk, chiffon and satin, showed off the female figure to great advantage.

A tall, slender figure was most sought after, and long trousers that many women wore accentuated the long lines and slim waists of the era.

The pin-ups of the World War II era such as the recently named 'Notorious Bettie Page', were preoccupied with curves. It became acceptable to show more than a little skin, and long legs were a must. Many pin-up girls (so named because posters of them were pinned up in male locker rooms and mechanic shops across the country) wore elaborate props instead of clothing to make their pictures acceptable for marketing to the masses.

Marilyn Monroe really took the pin-up era to another level and became an iconic beauty whose standard remains even today. Models, actresses, drag queens, even everyday women in modern times strive to attain her classic and timeless beauty. Though she was much larger than today's fashion models (some place her size as the equivalent of today's UK size 14), her body size and proportions especially are and, perhaps always will be seen as close to perfection. She was an icon and a standard of Hollywood beauty in her time and still is very much so today.

The swinging sixties saw a split in body image with so-called 'supermodels' leaning toward one end of the Body Mass Index and actresses leaning toward the other. Many actresses of the day (including Marilyn Monroe) were revered for their classical figures and their curvy shapes while high fashion began a trend that continues today...the thinner the better, even if you have to starve to death.

A return to natural beauty was the hallmark of 1970s female beauty. Women desired to attain a girl-next-door natural look that would affirm their increasing independence from and rejection of need for male approval. Television shows such as *Charlie's Angels* and *The Dukes of Hazzard* showcased women in unadorned yet still powerfully feminine roles.

Anyone who remembers the huge shoulder pads of the eighties TV shows *Dallas* and *Dynasty* will remember that bigger was always better. To emphasize the transition of women from the homemakers into the workplace where they became power players, clothing and fashion began to reveal a strikingly dramatic and powerful woman.

The female image of the 'noughties' is that of a physically fit, muscular powerful female. Beyonce, Shakira, Kylie Minogue are iconic female forms of the new century.

A normal body fat level for healthy females is around 25%. Many women attempt to reduce their percentage below this healthy level by dieting. This can have the effect of altering their secondary sexual characteristics. If the percentage drops below 18%, reproduction function may be compromised. This situation often opens the way for the use of performance-enhancing drugs.

Women who are insecure about their bodies are more likely to buy beauty products, new clothes, and diet aids. It is estimated that the diet industry alone is worth anywhere between 40 to a 100 billion dollars (U.S.) a year selling temporary weight loss 90-95% of dieters regain the lost weight. The performance-enhancing drug industry fits neatly and seamlessly into this space. This is also a multi- billion industry.

Research indicates that regular exposure to images of thin, young, air-brushed female bodies is linked to depression, loss of self-esteem and the development of unhealthy eating habits in women and adolescent girls.

Growing numbers of men and women use drugs to gain muscle, lose fat or otherwise improve their body appearance or athletic performance. Although these substances are sometimes called 'ergogenic' (performance-enhancing) drugs, they might equally be called 'body image' drugs, because many individuals take them simply to improve personal appearance, rather than to improve performance in a specific sport.

A study of female bodybuilders has concluded that this activity can be a dangerous activity for women who have or are at risk of developing eating or body image disorders because the bodybuilding community accepts as normal the compulsive dieting, self-preoccupation and concomitant substance abuse that are associated with these disorders.

In a further study, 65 out of the 75 study subjects reported extreme dissatisfaction with their bodies; 'muscle dysmorphia.' In this study the bodybuilders who were in top physical condition felt small and weak, despite their physicality being the opposite. In this study there were patterns of eating behaviour, gender role behaviour and body image disorder that caused profound effects on the social and occupational functioning of women bodybuilders. Women who held degrees in law, medicine or business, had abandoned these careers to pursue an all-consuming lifestyle of rigorous dieting and spending many hours at the gym in the pursuit of the perfect body.

Men and body image
Men have not escaped from concerns with their body image. In 1996, American men spent $500 million on male cosmetic surgery procedures; $300 million on procedures such as pectoral implants, chin surgery, and penis enlargement and $200 million on procedures such as liposuction and rhinoplasty (nose jobs).

In 1997, American men spent $4 billion on exercise equipment and health club memberships, $3 billion dollars on grooming aids and fragrances and $800million on hair transplants.

It does appear that men are growing increasingly concerned with the appearance of their body, and are willing to spend millions of dollars to enhance their physical image. The fitness and cosmetic surgery industries have discovered this new demographic and have developed marketing strategies specifically targeted to young men. And while most are not undergoing drastic cosmetic procedures, the rate of hazardous eating and eating behaviours related to body image concerns is increasing.

Research shows that today's college men are reporting greater levels of body dissatisfaction, and this is true for both gay and heterosexual men. Research at the University of Iowa health care in 2002 indicated that men associate their attractiveness with increased muscle definition, and are concerned about body shape (as opposed to weight) and increasing their muscle mass. This study also concluded that eating disorders in males typically involve a constant competition to stay more muscularly defined than other men. Disordered eating and exercising behaviours among men are associated with obsessive feelings of inadequacy, unattractiveness, and failure.

A study surveying one hundred current Anabolic steroid users was conducted in the early 2000s in New South Wales, Australia to determine the characteristics of anabolic-androgenic steroid (AAS) users. The study design was constructed to determine their motivations for use, and to examine the patterns and correlates of AAS use, with particular attention to homo/bi-sexual men.

This predominantly male sample (94%) included 27% of homo/bi-sexual men. Homo/bi-sexual users reported a different pattern of AAS use from the heterosexual users. They started using at a later age and used smaller quantities less frequently.

Homo/bi-sexual users were also more likely to identify as body image users and indicate that their motivation to use AAS on their first and most recent occasion was to improve appearance, although there were no significant differences between homo/bi-sexuals and heterosexuals in relationship to perceptions of body shape. The homo/bi-sexual men in this sample were also far more likely to have used a wide range of illicit drugs.

In the twenty-first century the ideal male body is growing steadily more muscular. Hypotheses regarding contemporary men's body image distress have been presented by researchers in the field of psychology. It appears that the media plays a significant role in this by presenting the public with unrealistic images of the ideal male body. Consider the following:

In 1999 Pope and his co researchers showed the changes that have occurred to the boys toy doll G.I. Joe. Joe as a doll barometer of men's body image has changed over the past twenty years. Today's G.I. Joe has grown more muscular and currently has sharper muscle definition, including statuesque biceps; quite different to the 1970s small thin soldier.

The world of the top shelf magazines have not escaped. The same research group showed in 2001 that a *Playgirl* centre-fold model of 1976 would need to shed twelve pounds of body fat and gain twenty-seven pounds of muscle to be a centerfold of today.

In addition, the male body is increasingly being objectified and sexualized in popular print ads. For example, advertisements promoting weight-lifting, exercise products, and underwear present the model as dehumanized and the body is objectified.

Unattainable Beauty
Perhaps most disturbing is the fact that media images of female beauty are unattainable for all but a very small number of women. Researchers generating a computer model of a woman with Barbie-doll proportions, for example, found that her back would be too weak to support the weight of her upper body, and her body would be too narrow to contain more than half a liver and a few centimetres of bowel. A real woman built that way would suffer from chronic diarrhoea and eventually die from malnutrition. The manufactures of Barbie estimated that 99% of girls aged three to ten years old own at least one Barbie doll. Therefore a significant proportion of the female child

population is being subjected to unrealistic and unattainable body image ideals.

Teenage Girls

Several studies, such as one conducted by Marika Tiggemann and Levina Clark in 2006 entitled 'Appearance Culture in Nine to Twelve-Year-Old Girls: Media and Peer Influences on Body Dissatisfaction' indicate that nearly half of all pre-adolescent girls wish to be thinner, and as a result have engaged in a diet or are aware of the concept of dieting.

In 2003, *Teen Magazine* reported that 35% of girls aged six to twelve years-old have been on at least one diet, and that 50-70% of normal weight girls believe they are overweight. Overall research indicates that 90% of women are dissatisfied with their appearance in some way. Television and movies reinforce the importance of a thin body as a measure of a woman's worth. Canadian researcher Gregory Fouts reports that over three-quarters of the female characters in TV situation comedies are underweight, and only one in twenty are above average in size. Heavier actresses tend to receive negative comments from male characters about their bodies. Of these negative comments, 80% are followed by canned audience laughter. Hence teenage girls are facing a constant bombardment of messages to be thin. In Madrid, one of the world's biggest fashion capitals, ultra-thin models were banned from the runway in 2006. Furthermore Spain has recently undergone a project with the aim to standardize clothing sizes through using a unique process in which a laser beam is used to measure real life women's bodies in order to find the most true to life measurement.

Unfortunately advertising rules the marketplace and in advertising thin is 'in'. Twenty years ago, the average model weighed 8% less than the average woman but today's models weigh 23% less. The barrage of messages about thinness, dieting and beauty tells 'ordinary' women that they are always in need of adjustment, and that the female body is an object to be perfected. Advertisers believe that thin models sell products. This message bombards their core audience: the teenage girl. Still, the number of real life women and girls who seek a similarly underweight body is epidemic, and they can suffer equally devastating health consequences. In 2006 it was estimated that up to 450,000 Canadian women were affected by an eating disorder.

The drive for muscularity in young men
The Drive for Muscularity – a concept touted by American psychologist Dr. Don McCreary in 2000 represents an individual's perception that he is not muscular enough, and that bulk should be added to his body frame.

Research shows that young men tend to see themselves as thinner and less muscular than they actually are. In contrast to women with body image concerns, who typically seek to shed pounds and achieve a specific body weight, men with body image concerns want to bulk up. Because men are socialized not to discuss their body image concerns, their silent anguish may lead to feelings of isolation, distress, depression, and anxiety. 2005 research by Dr. McCreary`s group has concluded that "the drive for muscularity" in young men has been associated with low self-esteem, neuroticism, and perfectionism. The drive for muscularity becomes pathological when it causes significant distress and interferes with social and occupational functioning. Any of the following signs are cause for concern:

1. Neglecting school, work, family, or friends to spend more time at the gym.
2. Persistent fear and anxiety of appearing too small.
3. The use of steroids or other performance-enhancing drugs.

Consequences of striving for the ideal body
Young men and women with a poor body image and a high drive for muscularity often have corresponding feelings of low self-esteem, anxiety, and depression. In addition, they may be more

at risk for abusing anabolic steroids, the health consequences of which are well documented. People who compare themselves to unrealistic images are likely to experience body image dissatisfaction, mental health issues, and threats to healthy physical functioning. Instead of striving for the perfect body, we should begin to identify the positive parts of ourselves and enjoy the body we have!

Why are standards of beauty being imposed on women, the majority of whom are naturally larger and more mature than any of the models in the magazines that they read? The roots, some analysts say, are economic. By presenting an ideal difficult to achieve and maintain, the cosmetic and diet product industries are assured of growth and profits. And it is no accident that youthfulness is increasingly promoted, along with thinness, as an essential criterion of beauty.

The advertising experts ensure that we feel badly as each *anno domini* strikes they have a pill or a potion, for a small consideration, that will turn back the clock and restore normality: youth, low body fat and bulging muscles. This is unattainable; it is unrealistic and unnatural. Women's magazines have ten and one-half times more ads and articles promoting weight loss than men's magazines do, and over three-quarters of the covers of women's magazines include at least one message about how to change a woman's bodily appearance, by diet, drugs exercise or cosmetic surgery. It is in this environment that performance-enhancing drug abuse for self image flourishes. The pressure to conform to fashion and the peer group is enormous. The American research group Anorexia Nervosa & Related Eating Disorders Inc. says that one out of every four college-aged women uses unhealthy methods of weight control. These include fasting, skipping meals, excessive exercise, laxative abuse, and self-induced vomiting. Children as young as six can be affected by this constant pressure to be thin.

The use of performance-enhancing drugs for reasons of body image may be one of the next great drug-abusing epidemics facing western society.

Young and old people are constantly being encouraged to conform to a particular body shape and type that is considered to be 'good', attractive, and therefore 'healthy'. This will open the gates to lifelong success and happiness. Young people in their thousands are being targeted to use performance-enhancing drugs to achieve this unnecessary and frequently unhealthy goal.

Unlike in the sporting community, body image (non performance enhancing) drug abuse is almost impossible to monitor and administer as there are no rules, no tests and no sanctions. The side effects of abuse, however, are as serious and significant as those who use these agents for reasons of sports performance.

Education and self-awareness of a normal body image is essential to redress this worsening problem. The experience of the ATLAS program of school drug education has taught us that early intervention by educating pre-teens and teens is the corner stone to influencing the next generation; this can prevent potential catastrophic consequences for this new form of social drug abuse.

Chapter 6
SUPPLEMENTS AND CREATINE

"Medicine sometimes snatches away health, sometimes gives it"
Ovid

A dietary supplement, also known as food supplement or nutritional supplement, is a preparation intended to supplement the diet and provide nutrients, such as vitamins, minerals, fiber, fatty acids, or amino acids, that may be missing or may not be consumed in sufficient quantity in a person's diet. Some countries define dietary supplements as foods, while in others they are defined as drugs or natural health products.

Food supplements in sport
Food supplements which include vitamins, mineral, herbals and homeopathic preparations are widely used in the society. Sportsmen and women also use these agents in an effort to enhance their performance and gain an edge over fellow competitors.

These products are not licensed and are therefore not liable to the strict regulations relating to labelling of constitutes substances which pertain in the pharmaceutical industry. The purity and consistency of these products is therefore in doubt. Some of these substances have been shown to contain substances which are not listed in the contents and may lead to positive performance enhancing drug tests. The manufacturers of many of these agents are aware of an athlete's desire for success, therefore the marketing of these products rely on personal endorsements and anecdotal evidence by patient rather then scientific data. There is little scientific evidence to suggest that these agents alone will improve athletic performance.

Athletic drug misuse is relatively easy to administer as there are specific banned substances, methods of detection and sanctions for infraction. The majority of athletes are aware of the rules and regulations related to the use of drugs in sport. Food supplementation is a much greyer area and can be the domain of sharp advertising on a vulnerable athlete. Athletes can be swayed by a slick sales pitch. As more drugs have been placed on the banned list for athletic performance, food supplements have gained a more prominent role in providing potential performance enhancement legally. This however, opens up a minefield to the supplementing athlete. Unlike medicines which are regulated by a statutory body in each country, there is no governing body to control and regulate the supplement industry. This raises the issue of supplement purity and safety. This concern was highlighted by research and undertaken at the Institute of Biochemistry, German Sports University situated in Cologne which showed that 14.8% of non-hormone nutrition supplements were contaminated by anabolic steroids. This was a European-wide phenomenon with the highest level of contaminations being reported in The Netherlands and Austria, by Schanzer in 2002 .

This underscores the major problem that supplementing athletes may imbibe a performance enhancing agent which may be banned, thus causing a doping infraction "unwittingly". With internet access and the availability of these agents through the internet, many athletes may unconsciously put their welfare and sporting future at risk by taking these agents.

Advising athletes regarding supplementation is always a difficult task. The best you can say about them is these products should be taken with caution and at the individual's own risk. The worst is that they may interfere with your health and well being. The truth lies somewhere between these two poles. Many of these agents have side effects which may compromise the individual's health and these agents may contain banned substances which would make the athlete vulnerable to sanction in view of the strict liability, zero tolerance of drug testing. In short every athlete is responsible for what is in his or her body. So if you take supplements you may run the risk of unwitting contamination with a banned or dangerous substance.

The history of supplements used in sport

Since the beginning of time, athletes have taken food and medicaments in an attempt to gain legal or illegal edges and advantages over fellow competitors. Administrators have almost always counseled against their use.

Philostratus called "the Athenian", was a Greek "sophist" In Ancient Greece, the sophists were a category of teachers who specialized in using the tools of philosophy and rhetoric for the purpose of teaching excellence or virtue to young statesmen and nobility. In his book "Gymnasticus", written around 220 AD, he writes an account of the Ancient Olympic Games. He notes the used "supplements" and advises that athletes should be freed from the "use of clay and mud and Erskine medicines".

Ancient strong men commonly trained by eating a pure meat diet. The earliest known example was Milo of Croton, the most famous Olympian of all time. Milo of Croton was a wrestler who lived in the 5th century BC. He won five gold medals and was known for prodigious feats of strength. He trained by lifting a calf each day. Then as the calf grew he lifted more each day and gradually gained strength. As a part of his lifting program he ate a pure meat diet. Thus, he was the first athlete to use modern training techniques of weight lifting and creatine supplementation.

In North America hunters such as the buffalo eating American Plains Indians, African Tribes, and Eskimos ate meat as almost their total energy source. Since meat contains one gram of creatine for each half pound of meat, these hunters consumed 3-5 grams of creatine per day depending of their total caloric need. This creatine dosage is similar to that recommended now by those who extol the use of this food supplement.

Strongmen, in the last and early part of this century, who demonstrated their strength by lifting heavy objects such as horses and anchors, often trained by eating a raw meat diet. The late world heavyweight boxing champion, Joe Frazier's, diet included chewing meat, swallowing the juice and then spitting out the rest.

This was despite the opinion then, as now among the medical and scientific professionals of the day, that there are no specific foods which will help elite athletes perform better. Despite significant research confirming this fact, the mainstay of all diets, for athletes and non athletes is healthy, balanced eating. Athletes over the centuries have always followed fashion and peers in a vain attempt to gain that critical edge.

Nutritional requirements of an athlete

The exercising body needs adequate energy substrates. Much research has gone into the actual daily requirements of specific activities. For example the energy requirement for an elite male athlete engaged in rowing is between 45-87 kcal/kg per day and between 29.5-46.3 kcal/kg for female athletes. In general, the requirement of all elite athletes who engage in daily activity is between three thousand and six thousand calories per day.

Researches indicated that the significant majority of athletes are consuming the recommended amount of food while in training. Vitamins and minerals play an important role in the nutrient metabolism. Physical activity may markedly increase the need for these elements however, their requirements are more than met by a normal balanced diet.

There is currently no evidence to suggest that vitamin and mineral supplementation can improve athletic performance in individuals who are eating a well-balanced diet. Athletes who eat a mixed diet adequate in calories are unlikely to be susceptible to deficiencies in any minerals or vitamins therefore adequate daily calorie intake would appear to be more important than selective supplementations of these agents.

Certain groups of athletes are susceptible to dietary deficiency. Runners, jockeys and wrestlers are particularly prone as these sports have a 'making weight' element. These individuals often have to be of a specific weight to be eligible to compete and therefore are likely to have a low calorie intake and as a result may not achieve the recommended daily intake of selective substances. Iron deficiency (anaemia) has been reported in these groups due to increased red cell break down and inadequate dietary intake of iron.

Iron supplementation should only be undertaken if true iron deficiency anaemia exists.

Aerobic exercise by its very nature causes the plasma volume to expand resulting in the dilution of the affected blood referred to as pseudo anaemia. This pseudo anaemia or athletic anaemia, which is simply due to dilution, does not require iron supplementation. It is a normal and natural response to intense aerobic exercise, and a similar physiological response of the body to natural stress that is also observed during pregnancy. Iron supplements by their very nature can be hazardous to health and are associated with a variety of side effects. One in a hundred individuals who have iron injected may be susceptible to a potentially fatal anaphylactic reaction. Similarly oral iron supplementation is associated with nausea and gastric upset and headaches. In extreme cases the chronic use of this supplement has been associated with the development of stomach cancer.

The acute effects of iron over dose are well known among the medical and nursing communities who have worked in Accident and Emergency Departments. Hardly a week would go by without a child presenting with an iron over dose. This usually occurs due to the child inadvertently consuming his or her mother's iron pills mistakenly thinking they are sweets. These children are often very ill with nausea, vomiting, dehydration and headaches. These seemingly harmless agents taken incorrectly can have significant unwanted effects.

The use of sports food supplements

Despite the scientific data which indicates that the majority of athletes have an adequate diet, 93% of all female running athletes in North America take vitamins and mineral supplementations. In a further study, 80% of females and 60% of male aerobic athletes report that they regularly use vitamins and mineral supplements while 100% of female and 90% of male anaerobic athletes also takes these agents. Athletes consume food supplements, in a belief that they will gain a performance enhancement. Administration of a physiologically inert substance, (a dummy pill or placebo) may help to improve performance, without the risk of side effects, if the athlete believes that this is probable.

Food supplements can be dangerous

Many if not all food supplements can cause side effects. Much of the short term reactions of these agents are known however, the long terms side effects are unknown due to paucity of research. Supplements used in sport are varied, and constantly changing, they include: Minerals, Protein, Vitamins, Hormones, Plant Extracts and Creatine

Minerals
Iron supplementation

Iron is a component of the red blood cells, and is involved in oxygen transportation. Reduced dietary intake has been observed in athletes who have to make weight, such as gymnasts and wrestlers, and in certain endurance-trained athletes, due to the mechanical trauma of exercise. The recommended daily intake for iron is 10 mg for men and 50 mg for women. The most appropriate way to ensure an adequate iron intake is to eat a balanced diet. Iron derived from animal foods is better absorbed than iron from plant foods. The iron in animal foods is described as haem iron, and eating a balanced diet that includes lean meat will give an adequate iron intake. Routine iron supplementation in the exercising athlete should be actively discouraged as this has many side effects, which can lead to morbidity and occasional mortality – anaphylaxis has been reported following iron supplementation use. The excess iron is not absorbed into the cells of the body but rather excreted through the kidneys, often resulting in discoloration of the urine. The analogy of pouring water into a glass which is full comes to mind when describing the body's response to excess iron supplementation. In normal circumstances the body simply does not absorb the excess iron. The actual substance can be toxic, and a variety of symptoms, from nausea and constipation to cardiac arrhythmias, have been reported as side effects of iron supplements. Any supplement should therefore be taken under medical supervision.

Iron supplementation is a very common practice in the sporting community. Iron supplementation has never been shown to improve performance in the non-anaemic state. One study in 1970 suggests that treadmill times can be improved by iron usage, but this animal study has never been replicated in humans. Despite this failure to replicate this single animal study, thousands of athletes take iron every day in the belief that it will improve their athletic performance.

Chromium
Chromium is a naturally occurring mineral. It is involved in normal glucose metabolism, insulin and fatty acid metabolism and in muscle. It is found in shellfish; however, chromium can easily be destroyed by food processing and cooking. The recommended daily intake of chromium is 50-200 mg in the sedentary population. It is suggested that the exercising athlete requires greater levels of chromium, as the increased insulin metabolism associated with exercise puts a greater demand on the body's chromium stores. The harder the exercise, the greater the chromium uses. Trivalent chromium is suggested to

be a glucose tolerance factor or a facilitator of normal glucose metabolism; this agent is not toxic, even in very large doses. Hexavalent chromium, however, is highly toxic, and is known to be carcinogenic.

Chromium in the form of chromium picolinate is a mineral supplement widely used by the exercising population. The chromium use by the athletic population is due to the suggested increase in insulin metabolism caused by exercise, which increases the body's chromium requirements. Research has indicated significant loss on training days as opposed to non-training days. Sources of chromium include organic forms such as chromium chloride; however, the biological activity of inorganic chromium is low.

Newer, more biologically active formulations have been developed, and the most commonly encountered variety is chromium picolinate, which was developed in Minnesota. This formulation has a significantly better absorption than the inorganic chromiums. Research among the athletic population has shown reduction in body fat percentage and increases in lean body mass in athletes who are supplemented with this mineral when compared to controls. Presently this mineral supplement is not banned by any of the regulating sports authorities. Its use, however, is in its infancy, and care with dosing and use should therefore be advised because its long-term effects have, as yet, not been fully established. Great care should be taken in using these supplements, and discussion of all nutrient supplementation should be encouraged between the athlete and the doctor because an athlete will often use an inappropriate formulation or dosage in an effort to gain a legal advantage over fellow competitors. The jury is still out in relation to this agent.

Zinc

Zinc is a component of many of the body's enzymes. Normal zinc metabolism is essential for the proper functioning of the immune system and of the reproductive system in the male, as zinc is essential for normal testosterone levels and sperm counts. The recommended daily intake of zinc is 15 mg; however, research has shown that the average 2850 calories American diet falls short of this recommended daily allowance by over 10%. Certain athletes may have an increased demand for zinc due to greater loss from red cell haemolysis and from losses in sweat. There may also be an increased demand for zinc by the exercising individual due to the increased fatty acid metabolism. There is research that suggests that exercise of itself may reduce the zinc status. In a similar way to iron deficiency, sports in which making weight is an integral component have a particular susceptibility to zinc deficiency due to an inadequate dietary intake (wrestling, gymnastics and dance). Distance runners also have an increased susceptibility to zinc deficiency due to foot strike haemolysis and blood loss from the bowel and bladder. Zinc toxicity occurs at a relatively low level, and is reported at an intake of 500 mg per day. Therefore, as with all supplementation, the athlete has to be carefully tutored and advised regarding supplementation with this potentially hazardous mineral.

Protein

Protein Supplementation is a common practice among the sporting community. Protein is an essential daily nutrient for both the sedentary individual and the athlete. Guidelines suggest that 15-30% of the daily nutritional intake should be in the form of protein. The actual daily intake can be calculated per kg or pound of body weight per day. The daily recommended intake for a sedentary adult is 0.9 g of protein per kg per day; competitive adult athletes should consume approximately 1.8 g of protein per kg of body weight per day, and growing teenagers should consume upwards of 2.2 g per kg of body weight per day. Many athletes follow a 'fad'-type dietary regimen and survive on a low saturated fat diet. Not only is protein sacrificed in this type of diet, but also iron and zinc, both essential daily nutrients. Most vegetarian diets can supply sufficient protein if individuals ensure that they eat a variety of foods that contain sufficient essential amino acids, such as beans and rice tofu. There are many protein supplements on the market. Protein supplementation of itself is probably safe. However they may be contaminated with other agents rendering them less than safe. A recent assessment of a major supplier of protein supplements have shown that their product was contaminated with a plant steroid, Beta Echysterone. The company was contacted by the news media for a response. Their press release was both interesting, and disturbing. It stated that the steroid found in their product was not a banned substance, and hence implied it was safe for human consumption. This is simply not so. The safety or otherwise of any food, plant or pharmacological agent can only be determined by scientific investigation, not by its presence or absence on a banned list. In this instance the manufacturer used the rules of elite sport to confer sham security to unsuspecting protein supplement users.

Antioxidants

Muscle power is generated by the conversion of adenosine triposphate (ATP) into energy. This can occur aerobically or anaerobically. ATP is generated aerobically by two processes:

1. Tetravalent reduction of oxygen with cytochrome C oxidase
2. Univalent reduction of oxygen

The second pathway produces free radicals during exercise; namely, superoxide free radicals, hydroperoxide free radicals and hydroxyl free radicals. These free radicals increase during exercise, and are associated with muscle damage after exercise. The hydroxyl free radicals continue to cause injury. The hydroxyl free radicals react with the fat in the muscle cell membranes in a process called lipid peroxidation; the damaged fats also become free radicals called peroxyl radicals. These do further tissue damage and produce further free radicals, which can result in an inflammatory chain reaction that may persist for many hours after exercise. The white blood cells, neutrophils, are then released to mop up the dead muscle cells. Following this, further free radicals are released. The net result is a significant free radical release after intense exercise, which leaves the body stiff, sore and unable to exercise properly for up to five days.

Antioxidants are the body's defence mechanism against free radicals. There are three main anti-oxidants:

1. Catalase, this neutralizes hydrogen peroxides

2. Superoxide dismutase (SOD), which destroys superoxide radicals.

3. Glutathione peroxidase an enzyme family with peroxidase activity whose main biological role is to protect the organism from oxidative damage

Vitamin C, vitamin E, selenium and coenzyme Q10 are also considered to have antioxidant properties. Vitamin E in particular has attained much public notoriety in the recent years as an antioxidant. It is thought to break the lipid per oxidation chain reaction by absorbing free radicals to form tocopherol and tocopheroxyl radicals. These tocopheroxyl radicals are neutralized by vitamin C, with subsequent regeneration of vitamin E. The recommended daily intake of Vitamin E is 10 mg per day, although it is suggested that the athletic requirement may be greater. Research to date, however, has indicated that oral vitamin E supplementation results in few side effects, even when the normal daily recommended allowance is exceeded. Selenium is also involved in an antioxidant effect. It is suggested that it acts synergistically with vitamin E and forms active sites for glutathione activity on lipid peroxide radicals.

The use of antioxidants in the athletic population is in its infancy, and great care and supervision is therefore essential when employing these agents. In particular, selenium can become very toxic at levels above 800 mg per day and N-acetyl cysteine is associated with the development of kidney stones if it is not used in association with vitamin C. These agents should be used under supervision.

Hormones
Melatonin
Melatonin is a hormone that is secreted by the pineal gland. Since 1995, this hormone has been used as an over-the-counter dietary supplement. It is used to treat a variety of medical ailments; however, there is very little scientific data to back up many of the claims relating to its use. Research has indicated that it can help individuals with mild to moderate sleep disorders, and it can also be helpful in fighting jet lag. It is classified as a dietary supplement, and therefore does not come under the regulation of the Food and Drug Administration Standards. Care would be advised when using this supplement.

Plant Extracts
Ginseng
The ginseng root has been used for centuries in Asia. There are over twenty plants that have ginseng each having varying effects. Some forms of ginseng have a stimulant-like effect and claim that they reduce fatigue. Ginseng is also claimed to be manifested in immune function as well as anti-aging. There does not appear to be any conclusive scientific evidence supporting these claims or that ginseng is effective in sporting performance. The ginseng root itself does not contain prohibited substance however, there have been instances in a product containing or bearing the name ginseng containing prohibited substances such as ephedrine and anabolic steroids. At the Seoul Olympic Games when Anti Doping was in its infancy, a British sprinter was sanctioned for using the stimulant ephedrine. His explanations to the anti-doping control agents

was that he had been taking ginseng medication to improve his performance believing that this agent was safe. He advised the doping officials that his dosing regime was to take one ginseng tablet before the 100 m and two tablets before the 200 m. The doping control agent remarked in his notes that it was just as well he was not in running the marathon because taking this amount of ginseng which was combined with ephedrine would have undoubtedly resulted in his demise to a cardiac event. Therefore, it is essential that if one is taking an agent such as ginseng that its purity is guaranteed.

Mahung
Mahung is a plant that contains the prohibited substance ephedrine.

Guarana
Guarana is a form of caffeine which is found frequently in herbal or nutritional supplements. Caffeine is a restricted substance which is prohibited when the concentration of caffeine and urine is greater than12 mcg/ml. Guarana is reported to contain much higher levels of caffeine however, the source of caffeine such as coffee and tea contain between 1-4% caffeine.

Vitamins
Vitamins are regularly consumed by athletes and non athletes. In high doses they can be harmful and result in vitamin toxicity, which can have a specific side effect profile.

Vitamin A
Large doses of vitamin A, over a prolonged period of time can cause headaches, diarrhoea, dry and itchy skin, hair loss, loss of appetite and kidney and liver failure.

Vitamin C
Although excess vitamin C is usually excreted in the urine, large doses can result in diarrhea, nausea and stomach cramps.

Vitamin D
Large doses of vitamin D can result in side effects such as weakness, thirst, increased urination, gastrointestinal upset and depression. Prolonged doses can cause calcium deposit in soft tissues, blood vessel walls and kidneys resulting in catastrophic effects.

Vitamin E
Large doses of vitamin E can result in abdominal pain and vomiting.

Vitamin B3
Large doses can result in itching, flushing and tingling in the fingers and hands.

Supplement legislation
Supplements containing vitamins or dietary minerals are included as a category of food in the Codex Alimentarius, a collection of internationally recognized standards, codes of practice, guidelines and other recommendations relating to foods, food production and food safety. These texts are drawn up by the Codex Alimentarius Commission, an organization that is sponsored by the Food and Agriculture Organization of the United Nations (FAO) and the World Health Organization (WHO).

Legislation in Europe
The Food Supplements Directive of 2002 requires that supplements be demonstrated to be safe, both in quantity and quality. By definition, vitamins and minerals are essential, i.e. the body cannot make them, so they must be obtained exogenously or from the diet, but excessive intakes can be harmful, notably vitamin A.

Consequently, only those supplements that have been proven to be safe may be sold without prescription. As a category of food, food supplements cannot be labelled with drug claims in the bloc but can bear health claims and nutritional claims. This law has caused great controversy among the twenty-seven member states of the E.U., many of whom argue that we should be free to choose what we put into our own bodies.

Legislation in the United States

In the United States, a dietary supplement is defined under the Dietary Supplement Health and Education Act of 1994 (DSHEA) as a product that is intended to supplement the diet and contains any of the following dietary ingredients:

- a vitamin
- a mineral
- a herb or other botanical (excluding tobacco)
- an amino acid
- a concentrate, metabolite, constituent, extract, or combination of any of the above.

Furthermore, it must also conform to the following criteria:

- intended for ingestion in pill, capsule, tablet, powder or liquid form
- not represented for use as a conventional food or as the sole item of a meal or diet
- labelled as a "dietary supplement"

The margins of food supplement and drugs can be blurred, as the definition is open to misinterpretation. The hormones DHEA (a steroid), pregnenolone (also a steroid) and the pineal hormone melatonin are marketed as dietary supplements in the U.S.

Regulation of sports supplements in the U.S.A.

The Food and Drug Administration (FDA) regulates dietary supplements as a category of foods, and not as drugs. While pharmaceutical companies are required to obtain FDA approval which involves assessing the risks and benefits prior to their entry into the market, dietary supplements do not need to be pre-approved by the FDA before they can enter the market.

Instead, manufacturers and distributors who wish to market dietary supplements that contain a "new dietary ingredient" must only notify the FDA beforehand.

There are different rules around the world for the regulation of food supplements with each jurisdiction having particular rules. For example creatine is a banned substance in France. Its sale or trafficking can result in penalties and fines. Throughout the rest of the E.U. it is sold openly and endorsed by many paid sports stars.

The internet circumvents the food supplement regulations. Almost anyone, anywhere in the world can obtain food and sports supplements from this source.

Nancy Clarke`s nutritional research of 1992 has shown that 92% of American female elite athletes take food supplements and vitamin agents. Up to 23% of all food or sport supplements are contaminated with performance enhancing agents. This can result in significant unconscious use of anabolic agents, growth hormones and stimulants, which have significant health consequences.

The purity and potential contamination by infection can be a particular problem. This is more frequent in illicit drugs and supplements.

The illicit sport supplements market is not regulated. Many of these agents are produced in 'Garage' pharmacies, such as occurred in the BALCO Scandal, where little or no quality control takes place putting the user in the way of both pharmacological and infective contamination.

Infected Supplements

Research has also confirmed cases of infection caused specifically by ingestion of contaminated substances. Cases of Hepatitis B; AIDS and Creutz Feldt Jacob Disease (Mad Cow) have all been reported. Anecdotal evidence suggests that these infections emanate from corpses in Eastern Europe. It was a frequent practice for unscrupulous morticians to harvest pituitary glands from dead bodies. When a quantity of these glands were assembled, they were crushed, spun down and transported to South America, where they were manufactured into pharmacy-like packaging, and sold as a growth hormone, or a combination of growth promoting anabolic agents.

Unfortunately these illegal agents did not undergo the normal microbial killing protocols that would be usual in the regulated pharmaceutical industry. Therefore these serious infections probably started off in the corpses in Russia, and ultimately ended up in shinny packaging in a European gym, consumed by unsuspecting young men and women, who wished to improve their physical fitness, but ultimately ended their lives by unconscious drug abuse.

Creatine

Creatine is a naturally occurring protein made up of amino acid (protein building block) that's found in meat and fish, and also made by the human body in the liver, kidneys, and pancreas. It is converted into creatine phosphate or phosphocreatine and stored in the muscles, where it is used for energy.

Creatine is an organic acid that occurs naturally in vertebrates and helps to supply energy to muscle and nerve cells. Creatine was identified in 1832 when Michel Eugène Chevreul discovered it as a component of skeletal muscle, which he later named creatine after the Greek word for flesh, Kreas.

In the human body, approximately half of the daily creatine (1g) is produced from three different amino acids:

- arginine
- glycine
- methionine

The rest is taken in from the diet; mainly from fresh fish and meat. 95% of creatine is later stored in the skeletal muscles, with the rest predominantly in the brain, heart, testes, inner ear and hair cells.

Creatine's main function is to transfer energy from the mitochondria to the myofibrils. The daily turnover rate of creatine is approximately two grams. This two gram deficit is only recovered by autosynthesis (synthesis in the body) up to a level of one gram a day or 50% of the body's daily requirements.

The remainder of the one gram that is lost every day comes from an exogenous dietary source. Research has indicated that supplementation of creatine can lead to an increase in total muscle creatine and also in the phosphocreatine. An upper limit of creatine in the muscle has been proposed at 160 mmol/kg.

Creatine uses in athletic performance and body image alteration

Creatine supplements are popular among body builders, recreational gym users and competitive athletes. It is estimated that Americans spend roughly fourteen million dollars per year on creatine supplements. The attraction of creatine is that it may increase lean muscle mass and is thought to enhance athletic performance, particularly during high-intensity, short-duration sports.

In the course of high intensity , short-duration exercise, such as lifting weights or sprinting, phosphocreatine is converted into ATP, a major source of energy within the human body.

Not all human studies have shown that creatine improves athletic performance. Nor does every person seem to respond the same way to creatine supplements. For example, people who tend to have naturally high stores of creatine in their muscles don't get an energy-boosting effect from extra creatine. Preliminary clinical studies also suggest that creatine's ability to increase muscle mass and strength may help combat muscle weakness associated with illnesses such as heart failure and muscular dystrophy.

Although not all clinical studies agree, some conducted in both animals and humans have shown that creatine supplements improve strength and lean muscle mass during high-intensity, short-duration exercises. In these studies, the positive results were seen mainly in young people, less than twenty years of age. Most human studies have taken place in laboratories, not on actual sports participants. Creatine does not seem to improve performance in exercises that requires endurance (like running) or in exercise that isn't repeated. There is some scientific evidence that taking creatine supplements can 'marginally' increase athletic performance in high-intensity anaerobic repetitive cycling sprints, but studies in swimmers and runners have been less than promising, possibly due to the weight gain. At best the jury is out on the actual physical benefit of creatine. Much of the perceived physical benefit may be due to the effects of contaminants in creatine, such as anabolic steroids and growth hormones.

Creatine in competitive sport
Although creatine is not banned by the World Anti-Doping Agency (WADA), The American National Collegiate Athletic Association (NCAA) or the International Olympic Committee (IOC), its use for athletic performance is controversial. The NCAA prohibits member schools from giving creatine and other muscle building supplements to their athletes, although it doesn't ban athletes from using it. The French Agency of Medical Security for Food (AFSSA) asserts that the use of

creatine supplements is "against the spirit of sportsmanship and fair competition" and is banned in that country.

One of the major concerns regarding creatine is purity. A German study from the University of Cologne showed a decade ago that 23% of sport food supplements are contaminated by other agents. These impurities strike to the core of the problem with creatine. These agents are often produced in 'garage' facilities. The industry is unregulated. Therefore it is not subjected to the rigours of the pharmaceutical industry. Site visits and good practice are not part of the day to day world of the bootleg sports supplement manufacturer. Hence if the system has been producing anabolic agents and growth hormones, the anovulent pill or other potions, and the system has not been thoroughly cleaned contamination can be passed onto a batch of creatine when this is being produced. The user may be ingesting an impurity from a previous production. An Australian study also confirms this notion as it indicated a significant percentage of creatine was contaminated by the female hormones that constitute the pill.

Pure creatine appears to be generally safe, assuming it is not contaminated. When it is taken at high doses there is the potential for serious side effects such as kidney damage and the risk of inhibiting the body's natural production of creatine. The author of the Australian study has had clinical experiences of young men suffering from transient cardiovascular side effects which seem to be as a direct result of creatine use and sudden cessation of use.

Also of concern is the marketing of creatine-containing supplements directly at teenaged children, with claims about changing one's body with little effort. One survey conducted with college students found that teen athletes frequently exceed the recommended loading and maintenance doses of creatine. Meanwhile, neither safety nor effectiveness in those under nineteen has ever been tested.

There is also greater concern that the use of substances such as creatine may act as a portal of entry for more serious drugs. Many of the websites that sell creatine also sell anabolic agents; growth hormones and blood boosters. Once you enter these sites you are one click away from purchasing the more powerful and dangerous agents. Therefore creatine use in the school-going population should be actively discouraged.

Medical uses of creatine
Creatine supplementation has been, and continues to be, investigated as a possible therapeutic approach for the treatment of muscular, neuromuscular, neurological and neurodegenerative diseases (arthritis, congestive heart failure, Parkinson's Disease, disuse atrophy, gyrate atrophy, McArdle's Disease, Huntington's Disease, miscellaneous neuromuscular diseases, mitochondrial diseases, muscular dystrophy). There is some specific data that indicates some therapeutic uses:

Heart disease
A preliminary clinical study suggests that creatine supplements may help lower levels of triglycerides (fats in the blood) in men and women with abnormally high concentrations of triglycerides.

In a few clinical studies of people with congestive heart failure, those who took creatine (in addition to standard medical care) saw improvement in the amount of exercise they could do before becoming fatigued, compared to those who took a placebo. Getting tired easily is one of the major symptoms of congestive heart failure. One clinical study of twenty people with congestive heart failure found that short-term creatine supplementation in addition to standard medication lead to an increase in body weight and an improvement of muscle strength.

Creatine supplementation shows promising therapeutic advantage in relation to congestive cardiac failure in the mitochondrial myopathies, which is heart failure associated with a genetic defect in energy production in the heart muscle. Creatine has also been reported to help lower levels of homocysteine. Homocysteine is a marker of potential heart disease, including heart attack and stroke.

Chronic Obstructive Pulmonary Disease (COPD)
In one double-blind study, people with COPD who took creatine increased muscle mass, muscle strength and endurance, and improved their health status compared with those who took placebo. They did not increase their exercise capacity. More studies are needed to see whether creatine has any benefit for people with COPD.

Geriatric population
Creatine has also been used in the geriatric population and a 2000 report has shown an improvement in the quality of life for patients. Research into cause and effect is still ongoing.

Muscular dystrophy
People who have muscular dystrophy may have less creatine in their muscle cells, which may contribute to muscle weakness. One study found that taking creatine resulted in a small improvement in muscle strength. However, other studies have found no effect.

Parkinson's Disease
People with Parkinson's disease have decreased muscular fitness including decreased muscle mass, muscle strength, and increased fatigue. A small clinical study found that giving creatine to people with Parkinson's Disease improved their exercise ability and endurance. In another clinical study, creatine supplementation improved patients' moods and led to a smaller dose increase of drug therapy. More research is needed in this area.

Ocular Disease
Research is ongoing to assess the uses of creatine in treating an eye disorder such as glaucoma, macular degeneration, diabetic retinopathy, cataracts, dry eye, iritis, retinitis pigmentosa. Creatine has also been trialled in ophthalmology for conditions such as gyrate atrophy of the choroids and retina. The research is variable on the benefits in all but macular degeneration.

Dietary sources of creatine
About half of the creatine in our bodies is made from other amino acids in the liver, kidney and pancreas, while the other half comes from foods we eat. Wild game is considered to be the richest source of creatine, but lean red meat and fish (particularly tuna, herring, and salmon) are excellent sources. A number of methods for ingestion exist - as a powder mixed into a drink, or as a capsule or caplet. Once ingested, creatine is highly bioavailable, whether it is ingested as the crystalline monohydrate form, the free form in solution, or even in meat.

Statuesque Muscle Development
Creatine increases what is known as cell volumization by drawing water into muscle cells, making them large. This intracellular retention often results in statuesque muscle development. The muscles may look bigger; but are not any stronger. There is only an increase in water weight. An increase in water weight can make you appear to be bloated. And because your muscle will retain more water, they might feel softer to the touch. This is one of the reasons that the American National Football League and Basketball League actively ban creatine, and discourage the use of this agent. This increase in intercellular water is also considered to be associated with the increased incidence in muscle tears in those who use this supplement.

Mood Swings
Research on the potential psychological side effects of creatine use is limited. Bodybuilding website resources however identify this as a potential problem. "Though creatine supplements

allegedly do not have side effects, users have reported that they suffer from mental mood swings, anger, and increased aggressive behavior, among other short term side effects. Anger and aggressive behavior seems to be one of the most reported side effects among users, both male and female."

Possible drug interactions associated with creatine
If you are currently being treated with any of the following medications, you should not use creatine without first talking to your doctor and prescriber.

Non-steroidal anti-inflammatory drugs (NSAIDs)
Creatine may increase the risk of damage if taken with these pain relievers, such as ibuprofen (Neurofen) or naproxen. Both NSAIDS and creatine are metabolised by the kidneys. Hence they may over load and damage these organs.

Caffeine
Caffeine may inhibit the body's ability to use creatine. Taking creatine and caffeine may increase risk of dehydration. Using creatine, caffeine, and ephedra is a combination that can be used in sports supplements. These agents taken together will cause dehydration and there are concerns therefore regarding an increased risk of heat exhaustion in susceptible individuals during intensive activity.

Diuretics (water pills)
Taking creatine with diuretics may increase the risk of dehydration and kidney damage.

Cimetidine (Tagamet)
Taking creatine while taking Tagamet may increase the risk of kidney damage.

Probenicid
Taking creatine while taking probenecid (a drug used to treat gout) may increase the risk of kidney damage.

Creatine and Supplement contamination with Beta Ecdysterone

Beta Ecdysterone is also called twenty hydroxyecdysone is described as a naturally occurring steroid found in plants and insects. In insects, this steroid controls various biological processes including the progression between larval stages.

This agent is marketed as a naturally occurring anabolic steroid and is found in certain food supplements. It came to prominence when it was found in protein containing body building supplements and has also been found in certain formulations of creatine.

Research is very limited on the use of this agent. However, it is thought to promote protein synthesis thereby building muscles without interfering with testosterone levels. Little research has taken place to identify the side effect profile. Great concern however exists among the medical community in the use of this agent as a contaminant or indeed as an actual component of the various protein and creatine supplements. If it is in fact a true steroid, then it should only be administered under appropriate medical license. This agent underscores the contaminative problems with food supplementations and sports supplementation.

Should you supplement with creatine?

Creatine is sold in a variety of forms, including creatine monohydrate and creatine ethyl ester. They are sold as a guaranteed method of increasing muscle mass and strength. The bodybuilding and advertising community repeatedly speak the mantra that creatine monohydrate is the most cost-effective dietary supplement in terms of muscle size and strength gains. Arnold Schwarzenegger, former Governor of the state of California, confirms this premise in writing in the publication The New Encyclopedia of Modern Bodybuilding. This is no great surprise considering this is a multi-million dollar a year business. The truth is somewhat short of the claims.

Creatine does have some positive effects. Very few of these appear to relate to athletic performance. Medical science continues to research into the possible benefits of this supplement in the treatment of a variety of diseases. The side effect profile is also uncertain.

There is much evidence as to the short term side effects, most of which are not catastrophic. Disaster looms for the user in the short term if the creatine is impure or contaminated in any way. These contaminations can be both pharmacological (with the potential of drug side effects) or ineffective (with the potential of life threatening diseases such as AIDS, Hepatitis and Mad Cow Disease).

The jury is out as to the long term effect of this agent. In France concerns exist as to the potential "mutogenic effect" (precancerous) of non supplemental creatine use. This creatine is derived from various types of cooked offal, red meat, and kidney meat.

The concerns about creatine mimic those that were raised in the 1960s and 70s about another "safe" plant extract: Tobacco. It was only in the 70s when the Hill and Doll study categorically confirmed the association between Tobacco, heart disease and lung cancer that people sat up and took notice. Up to that point advertisers, paid sports champions and movie stars promoted the use of this "plant extract" that ultimately killed millions of users.

The advantages to the user are at best small, the potential dangers huge. Hence creatine use should be actively discouraged.

Supplement use in Sport
The practice of sports supplementation is fraught with danger. These agents are promoted as a means of clean performance enhancement. The pure supplements do not appear to provide a performance enhancement and significant proportions are contaminated with banned substances.

Both the pure and contaminated products can be harmful if used inappropriately. Adequate balanced dietary intake will deal with any real or apparent extra requirements for exercising athletes. For these reasons, supplementation used in sports should be discouraged. These agents should not be endorsed by sporting agencies and users should be constantly reminded that they are taking these agents at their own risk and if they are found to test positive as a result of supplementation, the responsibility of a positive finding is theirs and theirs alone as they must be responsible for all substances that they put in to their own bodies.

Chapter 7

ANABOLIC STEROIDS

"Do not use a hatchet to remove a fly from your friend's forehead" Chinese Proverb

Introduction

Androgenic Anabolic steroids (AAS) are synthetic substances similar to the male sex hormone testosterone. They are taken orally or are injected. The substances are known by the street names 'Juice', 'Gym Candy', 'Pumpers', 'Stackers' to name but a few. The word anabolic comes from the Greek anabolein, 'to build up', and the word androgenic from the Greek andros, 'man' + genein, 'to produce'.

Anabolic steroids officially known as anabolic-androgenic steroids (AAS) are drugs which mimic the effects of the male steroids testosterone and dihydrotestosterone. They increase protein synthesis within cells, which result in the buildup of cellular tissue (anabolism), especially in muscles. They also have androgenic and virilizing properties, including the development and maintenance of masculine characteristics such as the growth of the vocal cords and body hair.

They were first isolated, identified and synthesized in the 1930s, and are now used therapeutically in medicine to stimulate bone growth and appetite, induce male puberty, and treat chronic wasting conditions, such as cancer and AIDS.

There is much argument as to when AAS entered the sporting arena. While these agents were available in the 1930s, they were not used in the Berlin Olympics of 1936, but they made their debut in Helsinki at the 1952 games when the Russian team swept the medal boards.

It is acknowledged that AAS, in the presence of adequate diet, can contribute to increases in body weight, often as lean mass increases, and that the gains in muscular strength achieved through high-intensity exercise and proper diet can be additionally increased by the use of AAS in some individuals.

Some health risks can be produced by long-term use or excessive doses of anabolic steroids. These effects include harmful changes in cholesterol levels (increased low-density lipoprotein and decreased high-density lipoprotein), acne, high blood pressure, liver damage, and dangerous changes in the structure of the left ventricle of the heart; which can result in cardiomyopathies (swelling and ineffective pumping of the heart).

More recent research has confirmed that chronic anabolic steroid abuse is associated with psychological and behavioral changes, the most florid being 'Roid Rage'. There is also significant evidence for the increased use of AAS for cosmetic reasons, also among the non-athletic college population.

The use of AAS in sport to gain an advantage is considered cheating. Their use is referred to as 'doping' and banned by all major sporting bodies. AAS's were banned in 1976. Therefore it is considered reasonable to assume many sporting champions would have used these agents between 1952 and 1975.

Detection of AAS in an athlete will result in penalties which can run from disqualification from the sport for a period of time to a life time ban, for repeated abuse. For many years the AAS have been by far the most detected doping substances picked up in WADA accredited laboratories. AAS are controlled substances, there is usually a black market in which smuggled or even counterfeit drugs are sold to users.

Many of the illegal steroids are smuggled in from other countries, illegally diverted from U.S. and European pharmacies, or synthesized in secret unregulated laboratories. Estimates show that there are more than four hundred million dollars worth of black-market (illegal) sales of steroids per year worldwide.

Athletes and others abuse anabolic steroids to enhance performance and also to improve physical appearance. Anabolic steroids are taken orally or injected, typically in cycles of weeks or months (referred to as 'cycling'), rather than continuously. 'Cycling' involves taking multiple doses of steroids over a specific period of time, stopping for a period, and starting again. In addition, users often combine several different types of steroids to maximize their effectiveness while minimizing negative effects. This is referred to as 'stacking'.

Incidence of anabolic steroid abuse

It is difficult to establish the exact number of AAS abusers. Research is often difficult to conduct as it is usually an underground activity. A 2002 British Medical Journal publication has suggested that 9.1% of male and 2.3% of female gym users in England and Scotland admitted to AAS use.

In North West England, 50% of hardcore gym users, 13% of fitness gym users and 31% of mixed gym users admitted to AAS abuse.

A study to assess the prevalence of use of anabolic-androgenic steroids and other presumed performance-enhancing drugs in school-aged Canadians was also staggering. More than 83,000 young Canadians (2.8% of the respondents) are estimated to have used anabolic-androgenic steroids in the year before the survey. Of those taking such drugs, 29.4% reported injecting them; and of these 29.2% reported sharing needles in the course of injecting anabolic-androgenic steroids. Significant numbers of the respondents reported using other substances (caffeine 27%, extra protein 27%, alcohol 8.6%, painkillers 9%, stimulants 3.1%, and 'doping methods' 2.3% and beta-blockers 1%) in attempts to improve sport performance.

The use of anabolic-androgenic steroids is more widespread than may have been assumed and is often accompanied by high-risk needle-sharing. Anabolic-androgenic steroid use is often intended to alter body shape, as opposed to accentuating sport performance.

In North America the National Institute of Drug Abuse (NIDA) funded research in 2008 entitled 'Monitoring the Future Study' showed that 0.9% of eighth graders, 0.9% of tenth graders, and 1.5% of twelfth graders had abused anabolic steroids at least once in the year prior to being surveyed. This statistic is frightening!

History of anabolic steroids
The use of gonadal steroids pre-dates their identification and isolation. Medical use of testicle extract began in the late nineteenth century while its affects on strength were still being studied. The isolation of gonadal steroids can be traced back to 1931 when Adolf Butenandt, a chemist in Marburg, purified fifteen milligrams of the male hormone androstenone from tens of thousands of liters of urine. This steroid was subsequently synthesized in 1934 by Leopold Ruzicka, a chemist in Zurich. In the 1930s it was already known that the testes contained a more powerful androgen than androstenone, and three groups of scientists, funded by competing pharmaceutical companies in the Netherlands, Nazi Germany and Switzerland, raced to isolate it.

This hormone was first identified by Karoly Gyula David, E. Dingemanse, J. Freud and Ernst Laqueur in a May 1935 paper entitled: 'Crystalline Male Hormone from Testicles (Testosterone)'. They named the hormone testosterone, from the stems of testicle and sterol, and the suffix of ketone. The chemical synthesis of testosterone was achieved in August that year, when Butenandt and G. Hanisch published a paper describing 'A Method for Preparing Testosterone from Cholesterol.'

Only a week later, the third group, Ruzicka and A. Wettstein, announced a patent application in a paper on 'The Artificial Preparation of the Testicular Hormone Testosterone (Androsten-3-one-17-ol).'

Ruzicka and Butenandt were offered the 1939 Nobel Prize for Chemistry for their work, but the Nazi government forced Butenandt to decline the honor, although he accepted the prize after the end of World War Two.

Clinical trials on humans, involving either oral doses of methyltestosterone or injections of testosterone propionate, began as early as 1937. Testosterone propionate is mentioned in a letter to the editor of Strength and Health Magazine in 1938; this is the earliest known reference to an anabolic steroid in a U.S. weightlifting or bodybuilding magazine. There are often reported rumors that German soldiers were administering anabolic steroids during the Second World War, the aim being to increase their aggression and stamina, but these are, as yet, unproven. Adolf Hitler himself, according to his physician, was injected with testosterone derivatives to treat various ailments.

AAS were used in experiments conducted by the Nazis on concentration camp inmates, and later by the allies attempting to treat the malnourished victims that survived Nazi camps.

Development of synthetic AAS

Chemical structure of the synthetic steroid Methandrostenolone (Dianabol). 17α-methylation (the OH in the upper right corner) enhances oral bioavailability.

The development of muscle-building properties of testosterone was pursued in the 1940s, in the Soviet Union and in Eastern Bloc countries such as East Germany, where steroid programs were used to enhance the performance of Olympic and other amateur weight lifters. In response to the success of Russian weightlifters, the U.S. Olympic Team physician, Dr. John Zeigler, worked with synthetic chemists to develop an anabolic steroid with reduced androgenic effects.

Zeigler's work resulted in the production of methandrostenolone, which Ciba Pharmaceuticals marketed as Dianabol. The new steroid was approved for use in the U.S. by the Food and Drug Administration (FDA) in 1958. It was most commonly administered to burn victims and the elderly.

The drug's off-label users were mostly bodybuilders and weight lifters. Although Zeigler prescribed only small doses to athletes, he soon discovered that those who abused Dianabol suffered from enlarged prostates and shrunken testes.

AAS were placed on the list of banned substances by the IOC in 1976. A decade later, the committee introduced 'out-of-competition' doping tests because most of the abusers used AAS in their training period rather than during competition. Different anabolic steroids have different effects

Testosterone and its synthetic counterpart anabolic steroid are called C-19 steroid hormones. They are produced in the body of males and females from cholesterol. The compounds are made up of four chemical rings; called benzene rings. Other compounds are added and subtracted to these four rings to make different versions of AAS.

There are potentially thousands of different anabolic steroids. AAS are altered to have either different clinical and physiological effects or to evade detection by the drug detection agencies. The most famous in recent years was THG produced by the company BALCO in California. This agent was called "clear" as its formulation was considered to be undetectable to drug testing methods, due to an alteration in the chemical element on one of the benzene rings that make up an anabolic steroid. In that instance the alteration was at a specific location on the fourth ring referred to as the 17-alpha position.

Three major ideas governed modifications of testosterone into a multitude of AAS. They were derived from chemical modifications of the compound by the chemical reactions of alkylation; etherification or alteration of the benzene ring structure:

1. Alkylation at 17-alpha position with methyl or ethyl group created orally active compounds because it slows the breakdown of the drug by the liver.
2. Etherification of testosterone and nortestosterone at the 17-beta position allows the substance to be administered by injection and increases the duration of effectiveness because agents soluble in oily liquids may be present in the body for several months.
3. Alterations of the ring structure were applied for both oral and injected agents seeking to obtain different anabolic to androgenic effect ratios.

The androgenic to anabolic ratio of an AAS is an important factor when determining the clinical application of these compounds. Compounds with a high ratio of androgenic to anabolic effects are the drug of choice in androgen-replacement therapy (e.g. treating hypogonadism in males), whereas compounds with a reduced androgenic anabolic ratio are preferred for anemia, osteoporosis, and to reverse protein loss following trauma, surgery or prolonged immobilization.

Determination of androgenic to anabolic ratio is typically performed in animal studies, which has led to the marketing of some compounds claimed to have anabolic activity with weak androgenic effects. This disassociation is less marked in humans, where all anabolic steroids have significant androgenic effects.

A commonly used protocol for determining the androgenic to anabolic ratio, dating back to the 1950s, uses the relative weights of prostate and the pelvic levator ani muscle. In the early nineties this procedure was standardized as the Hershberger Assay. The different AAS, with the different anabolic to androgenic ratios have different clinical and physical effects. These are listed in the following table:

Anabolic and androgenic effects of anabolic steroids

Relative androgenic:anabolic activity in animals	
Preparation	Ratio
Testosterone	1:1
Methyltestosterone	1:1
Fluoxymesterone	1:2
Oxymetholone	1:3
Oxandrolone	1:3–1:13
Nandrolone decanoate	1:2.5–1:4

Anabolic steroid effect on physical performance

As the name suggests, anabolic-androgenic steroids have two different, but overlapping, types of effects: anabolic, meaning that they promote anabolism (cell growth), and androgenic (or virilizing), meaning that they affect the development and maintenance of masculine characteristics.

Some examples of the anabolic effects of these hormones are; increased protein synthesis from amino acids, increased appetite, increased bone remodeling and growth, and stimulation of bone marrow, which increases the production of red blood cells. Through a number of mechanisms anabolic steroids stimulate the formation of muscles cells and hence cause an increase in the size of skeletal muscles leading to increased strength.

The androgenic effects of AAS are numerous. Processes affected include pubertal growth, sebaceous gland oil production, and sexuality (especially in fetal development). Some examples of virilizing effects are growth of the clitoris in females and the penis in male children (the adult penis does not grow even when exposed to high doses of androgens), increased growth of androgen-sensitive hair (pubic, beard, chest, and limb hair), increased vocal cord size, deepening the voice, increased libido, suppression of natural sex hormones, and impaired production of sperm.

Medical and ergogenic uses of Anabolic steroids
Since the discovery and synthesis of testosterone in the 1930s, anabolic steroids have been used by physicians for many purposes, with varying degrees of success.

Bone marrow stimulation
For decades, anabolic steroids were the mainstay of therapy for hypoplastic anemias due to leukaemia or kidney failure, especially aplastic anemia. Anabolic steroids have largely been replaced in this setting by synthetic protein hormones such as erythropoietin that selectively stimulate blood cell precursors.
Growth stimulation
Anabolic steroids can be used by pediatric endocrinologists to treat children with growth failure. However, the availability of a synthetic growth hormone, which has fewer side effects, makes this a secondary treatment.

Stimulation of appetite
Stimulation of appetite and preservation and increase of muscle mass: Anabolic steroids have been given to people with chronic wasting conditions such as cancer and AIDS.

Induction of male puberty
Androgens are given to many boys distressed about extreme delay of puberty. Testosterone is now nearly the only androgen used for this purpose and has been shown to increase height, weight, and fat-free mass in boys with delayed puberty.

Male contraception
Testosterone enanthate has frequently been used as a male contraceptive and it is thought that in the near future it could be used as a safe, reliable, and reversible male contraceptive.

Lean body mass
Anabolic steroids have been found in some studies to increase lean body mass and prevent bone loss in elderly men. However, a 2006 placebo-controlled trial of low-dose testosterone supplementation in elderly men with low levels of testosterone found no benefit on body composition, physical performance, insulin sensitivity, or quality of life.

Treatment of male libdo
Anabolic steroids are used in hormone replacement therapy for men with low levels of testosterone and are also effective in improving libido for elderly males.

Gender Identity Disorder
Anabolic steroids are often used to treat Gender Identity Disorder by producing secondary male characteristics, such as a deeper voice, increased bone and muscle mass, facial hair, increased levels of red blood cells and clitoral enlargement in female-to-male transgender patients.

Body composition and strength improvements
A review spanning more than three decades of experimental studies in men found that body weight may increase by 2–5 kg as a result of short term (less than ten weeks) AAS use, which may be attributed mainly to an increase of lean mass. Animal studies also found that fat mass was reduced, but most studies

in humans failed to elucidate significant fat mass decrements. The effects on lean body mass have been shown to be dose dependent. Both muscle hypertrophy and the formation of new muscle fibers have been observed.

The upper region of the body (thorax, neck, shoulders and upper arm) seems to be more susceptible to AAS than other body regions because of the predominance of androgen receptors in the upper body. The largest difference in muscle fiber size between AAS users and non-users was observed in type I muscle fibres of the vastus lateralis and the trapezius muscle as a result of long-term AAS self-administration. After drug withdrawal the effects fade away slowly, but may persist for more than six to twelve weeks after cessation of AAS use.

The same review observed strength improvements in the range of 5-20% of baseline strength, largely depending on the drugs and dose used as well as the administration period. Overall, the exercise where the most significant improvements were observed was the bench press.

In 1996 a randomized controlled trial published in the New England Journal of Medicine demonstrated however that even in novice athletes a ten week strength training program accompanied by testosterone enanthate at 600 mg/week may improve strength more than training alone does. The same study found that dose was sufficient to significantly improve lean muscle mass relative to placebo even in subjects that did not exercise at all. A 2001 study by the same author showed that the anabolic effects of testosterone enanthate were highly dose dependent.

Adverse effects of anabolic steroids
Abuse of anabolic steroids has been linked with many health problems. They range from unattractive to life threatening and include:

Minor side effects
- Acne and cysts
- Breast growth and shrinking of testicles in men
- Voice deepening and growth of body hair in women

Potentially fatal side effects
- Cardiovascular (heart problems, including heart attack)
- Liver disease, including cancer
- Aggressive behaviour (Roid Rage)
- Diabetes

Cardiovascular
Anabolic steroids can cause many adverse effects. Most of these side effects are dose-dependent, the most common being elevated blood pressure, especially in those with pre-existing hypertension, and harmful changes in cholesterol levels: some steroids cause an increase in LDL cholesterol and a decrease in HDL cholesterol.

Metabolic
Anabolic steroids have been shown to alter fasting blood sugar and glucose tolerance tests. Anabolic steroids such as testosterone also increase the risk of cardiovascular disease or coronary artery disease.

Skin
Acne is fairly common among anabolic steroid users, mostly due to stimulation of the sebaceous glands by increased testosterone levels. Conversion of testosterone to dihydrotestosterone (DHT) can accelerate the rate of premature baldness for males who are genetically predisposed, but testosterone itself can produce baldness in females.

Liver
High doses of oral anabolic steroid compounds can cause liver damage, as the steroids are metabolized in the hepatic and digestive system to increase their bioavailability and stability.

Glucose and Immunoglobulin's

Anabolic steroid abuse has been shown to increase insulin resistance and reduce glucose tolerance. This can lead to the development of Type II Diabetes. Synthetic anabolic steroids seem to have a greater effect on diabetic risk, rather than the naturally occurring testosterone which can be converted to estrogen.

The Immunoglobulins IgA and IgG which are both associated with the immune response can also be reduced during anabolic steroid abuse.

Tendon Injury

There have been several reports on the higher incidence of tendon injuries in athletes who abuse anabolic steroids. This is due to an overall reduction in the plasticity and function of tendons. Tendons are made of collagen. Anabolic steroids inhibit the production of normal collagen; less strong or morphologically deranged collagen being produced; which is more liable to injury and rupture. There is also a mismatch between tendon and muscle strength in the steroid user. Muscles in association with strength training increase their function and their ability to 'take weight'. This is not the case with tendons; which respond very slowly to strength regimes, and are unaffected by anabolic steroids. During activity the force that the muscle can tolerate, is not matched by the tendons and often rupture.

There are also sex-specific side effects of anabolic steroids. Development of breast tissue in males, a condition called gynecomastia (which is usually caused by high levels of circulating estrogen), may arise because of increased conversion of testosterone to estrogen by the enzyme aromatase. Reduced sexual function and temporary infertility can also occur in males. Another male-specific side effect which can occur is testicular atrophy; caused by the suppression of natural testosterone levels, which inhibits production of sperm (most of the mass of the testes is developing sperm). This side effect is temporary: the size of the testicles usually returns to normal within a few weeks of discontinuing anabolic steroid use as normal production of sperm resumes.

Female-specific side effects include increased growth of body hair, deepening of the voice, enlarged clitoris, and temporary changes in the menstrual cycles. When taken during pregnancy, anabolic steroids can affect fetal development by causing the development of male features in the female fetus and female features in the male fetus. There have also case reports of breast size reduction and persisting and irreversible masculinisation with significant psychological disturbance from gender identity issues.

Anabolic steroids and the adolescent
A number of severe side effects can occur if adolescents use anabolic steroids. For example, the steroids may prematurely stop the lengthening of bones (premature growth plate fusion through increased levels of estrogen metabolites), resulting in stunted growth. Adolescents who abuse AAS risk remaining short for the remainder of their lives if they take anabolic steroids before the typical adolescent growth spurt.

Other effects include, but are not limited to, accelerated bone maturation, increased frequency and duration of erections, and premature sexual development. Anabolic steroid use in adolescence is also correlated with poorer attitudes related to self care and health.

Other side effects can include alterations in the structure of the heart, such as enlargement and thickening of the left ventricle, which impairs its contraction and relaxation. Possible effects of these alterations in the heart are hypertension, cardiac arrhythmias, congestive heart failure, heart attacks, and an association with sudden cardiac death.

Psychiatric effects of anabolic steroids

Over the past thirty years there has been much anecdotal evidence to suggest a significant cause and effect relationship between anabolic steroid abuse and abnormal social behavior. In 2005 a review published in CNS Drugs determined that "significant psychiatric symptoms including aggression and violence, mania, and less frequently psychosis and suicide have been associated with steroid abuse. Long-term steroid abusers may develop symptoms of dependence and withdrawal on discontinuation of AAS".

High concentrations of AAS produce damaging effects on neurons, raising the spectre of possibly irreversible neuropsychiatric toxicity. Chronic low dose AAS use appears to be associated with a range of potentially prolonged psychiatric effects, including dependence syndromes, mood disorders, and progression to other forms of substance abuse, but the prevalence and severity of these various effects remains poorly understood.

There is no evidence to suggest that steroid dependence develops from therapeutic use of anabolic steroids when they are reasonably used to treat medical disorders. There are instances of AAS dependence which have been reported among weightlifters and bodybuilders who chronically administered supraphysiologic doses.

Mood disturbances (e.g. depression, [hypo-]mania, psychotic features) are likely to be dose-and drug-dependent, but AAS dependence or withdrawal effects seem to occur only in a small number of AAS users.

A thirteen month study, published in 2006 which involved three hundred and twenty body builders and athletes suggests that the wide range of psychiatric side effects induced by the use of AAS is correlated to the severity of abuse.

Aggression and hypomania associated with anabolic steroid abuse
From the mid 1980s onwards the popular press has been reporting 'roid rage' as a side effect of AAS. A 2005 review determined that some, but not all, randomized controlled studies have found that anabolic steroid use correlates with hypomania and increased aggressiveness.

A 2008 study on a nationally representative sample of young adult males in the United States found an association between lifetime and past-year self-reported anabolic-androgenic steroid use and involvement in violent acts, compared with individuals who did not use steroids. Young adult males who used anabolic-androgenic steroids reported greater involvement in violent behaviors.

A 1996 review examining the studies available at that time also found that these had demonstrated a link between aggression and steroid use, but pointed out that with estimates of over one million past or current steroid users in the United States at that time, an extremely small percentage of those using steroids appear to have experienced mental disturbance severe enough to result in clinical treatments or medical case reports.
A trial conducted in 2000 using testosterone cyprionate at 600 mg/week found that treatment significantly increased manic scores and aggressive responses on several scales. The drug response was highly variable, however, 84% of subjects exhibited minimal psychiatric effects, 12% became mildly hypomanic, and 4% (two subjects) became markedly hypomanic.

Depression and suicide associated with anabolic steroid abuse
The relationship between AAS use and depression is inconclusive. There have been anecdotal reports of depression and suicide in teenage steroid users, but little systematic evidence. A 1992 review found that anabolic-androgenic steroids may both relieve and cause depression, and that cessation or diminished use of

anabolic-androgenic steroids may also result in depression, but called for additional studies due to disparate data.

Anabolic steroid addiction

Recent research conducted by Dr. Ruth Wood, of the University Southern California has highlighted the potential for Anabolic steroids to be addictive. Most people who use anabolic steroids do so to enhance their physical performance, or their cosmetic appearance. Most abusers deny that steroids are addictive. Unlike other commonly abused drugs, such as cocaine and heroin the primary motivation for steroid users is not to get high, but rather to achieve enhanced athletic performance, increased muscle mass, and improve their body image.

In an animal study conducted at USC, hamsters were implanted with small cannulas for self-administration of commonly abused steroids into their brains. The animals then spent four hours per day in a chamber with access to two delivery mechanisms.

The animals showed a marked preference for the steroids testosterone, nandrolone and drostanolone, engaging the active delivery mechanism twice as often as the control. However, not all steroids are rewarding: hamsters did not voluntarily ingest the weak steroids stanozolol or oxymetholone. By isolating the animals, researchers were able to remove the possibility that the hamster's decision to take the drugs would be affected by any social or behavioral factors.

The research concluded that animals perceive the steroids to be rewarding demonstrating the drugs' potential for addiction. The researcher noted that the specific pattern of abuse demonstrated by hamsters suggests that a commonly held belief about steroids is true: rather than an acute high like that experienced by a cocaine or heroin user, steroid abuse participants experience a chronic, long-term sense of well-being. In essence steroid users feel better on the drugs than they do off of them.

"The findings demonstrate that anabolic steroids do have the potential to be addictive," Wood concluded. The research also concluded that psychiatrists and other mental health professionals should be aware of the finding, as men who use anabolic steroids to change their appearance may have a serious body image disorder and may and present to a health care provider with psychiatric symptoms.

There are also a number of reports of steroid craving, and of widespread fear, be it real or imaginary of what is referred to as 'muscle melt down' in those attempting to withdraw from steroid abuse. Nevertheless there is only one case report in the scientific literature of a female anabolic steroid abuser suffering from actual clinical dependency on the drug.

Anabolic steroid use and cocaine
U.K. research has indicated that 85% of anabolic steroid abusers also experiment with street drugs. These agents are also used in combination. According to the 2002 'Monitoring the Future Study' conducted by the University of Michigan, the lifetime incidence of steroid use among high school seniors (4.0%) was comparable to that for crack cocaine (3.8%) or heroin (1.7%). Combined use was also noted in this group.

An animal study using rats, in Finland suggests that the anabolic steroid nandrolone has a significant effect on the pleasurable properties of cocaine.

The study reported in the American Journal of Sports Medicine February 2010 shows that the anabolic steroid nandrolone potentiates the effects of cocaine. This was achieved by increasing the brains concentration of five hydroxytryptamine and dopamine resulting in an accentuation of the pleasurable properties of cocaine.

Furthermore, because neurochemical and behavioral responses were still attenuated after a fairly long recovery period, it seems that nandrolone may induce long-lasting damaging changes in the brains of the rats that were used in this study.

Anabolic Steroids and the Law

On the twenty-second of October 2004, President George W. Bush signed into law the Anabolic Steroid Control Act of 2004. This law took effect ninety days later. The law added twenty-six compounds to the existing ninety steroids that are classified as schedule three control substances. Possession of a single androgenic or other pro-hormone tablet such as androstenedione was from that day, considered to be a federal crime punishable by up to one year in jail. Distributing any of the ninety anabolic steroids will also be a felony punishable by up to five years imprisonment for a first offence. Of the twenty-six newly added compounds, androstenedione, which is the agent reportedly used by former baseball legends as it does not fall into the 1990 version of anabolic steroids is now also on the banned list from the federal law standpoint. The older steroids that were missed in the original federal law of 1990 were also added in the 2004 version. Interestingly, the new anabolic steroid control act of 2004 permitted the continued sale of DHEA as a dietary supplement.

There was also a significant change in the law in this definition of an anabolic steroid. No longer must it be proven that the compound is anabolic. The legislation states (the compound promotes muscle growth) has been removed from the statues and therefore it is no longer required by the law makers to prove that a compound is anabolic if it conforms to the chemical compound of these agents, then it is considered to be an anabolic steroid.

Tetrahydrogestrinone (THG) produced by the BALCO Laboratory in California known among the abusing athletic community as 'Clear' was also inserted in the list of 2004. It was considered that this change in the law also indicated a change in the whole anti-doping movement. The 1990 act was specifically geared towards preventing sports men and women abusing these substances. Society has changed significantly and performance-enhancing drug abuse is no longer the sole arena for athletes but rather non-athletes such as body builders and individuals who simply wish to improve their body physiology, function and form.

This act was an effort to alter the extraordinary dramatic rise in the use of illegal steroids among the non-sporting population and specifically steroid trafficking has been identified as a core area to try and reduce the spread of performance enhancing drug abuse.

The United Kingdom has added its weight behind the fight against performance enhancing drug abuse by altering legislation. In preparation for the 2012 London Olympic Games and in response to the pressure from the International Olympic Committee and the World Anti-Doping Agency (WADA), a steroid law revision occurred in the U.K. The new law added an additional twenty-four anabolic steroids and two non-steroidal agents to the existing list of fifty-four anabolic steroids and five growth hormones currently classified and scheduled for under controlled substance use and misuse of drugs act 1971. Concern however, still exist in anti-doping circles as the new law will still permit the personal use of anabolic steroids and the importation of anabolic steroids for personal use without any sanction under the United Kingdom law.

In September of 2010 the Advisory Council on the Misuse of Drugs (ACMD) published 'Consideration of the Anabolic Steroids', a report considering the misuse and harms of the substances.

The report was written following the ACMD's increasing concern at the numbers of anabolic steroid users. Among other findings, the report considers the potential harms to users due to the patterns of use and the presence of substandard and counterfeit steroids in the marketplace.

Professor Les Iversen, Chair of the ACMD, said that "The misuse and rising prevalence of anabolic steroids is a worrying development. Misuse carries significant risks, particularly for young people whose bodies are still developing".

The ACMD *report notes concerns around the following:*

1. Fifty thousand people aged between sixteen and fifty-nine years had used anabolic steroids in the last year (2009/2010 data)
2. Needle and syringe programmers have also observed a rise in steroid injectors.
3. Use of anabolic steroids by adolescents potentially disrupting the normal pattern of growth and behavioural maturation.
4. The majority of users inject anabolic steroids and are therefore potentially at risk of a number of serious harms including blood-borne viruses such as hepatitis B and C as a result of sharing used injecting equipment.
5. The ease of availability through transnational internet sites trading in these products.
6. The existence of substandard and counterfeit steroids within the marketplace posing a risk to users' health.

The ACMD made a number of recommendations to government and industry bodies.

It recommended that:

1. The legislative framework should be strengthened, primarily through reducing the availability of anabolic steroids.
2. The council considers that criminal prosecution should continue to be limited to illicit steroid dealers, suppliers, manufacturers and traffickers who profit from this trade as a Class C substance.

3. The council recommends improved intervention and education messages aimed at users.
4. Restriction to be placed on the importation and exportation exemption, namely personal custody on importation, thereby making online ordering of the substances illegal.
5. Ensure better availability of credible information and advice for users of anabolic steroids.

Steroid abuse and Needle Exchange Programmes:
In April of 2008, a review of Needle Exchange Programme with the United Kingdom was undertaken. It was alarming to see that the increasing number of steroid users entered the Needle Exchange Assistance Programme. The rate of steroid abuse has escalated as the highest users of the programme were no longer street drug abusers but rather steroid users. Reports confirmed that the increasing number of young people using steroids was due to aesthetic (body image) concerns.

The demographic of steroid users has also changed as well as their motivation. Among older users, the drugs are often taken as a means to open up non-academic job opportunities in manual fields. Particularly in manufacturing towns where manual workers found themselves unable to make a living in the older industries, they often trained as security staff, bouncers, police officers, to continue making living using their bodies. Unlike mining and manufacturing jobs for instance, these new careers did not develop appropriate physiques, (on the job) being a doorman requires a big build but the job itself is more likely to cultivate gut rather than shoulders; hence the rise of the gym culture and steroids.

It is fashion rather than function that motivates the younger generations to pump up. Ultimately what new users are concerned with is body image. It does not have anything to do with performance gain. It is usually about the aesthetic look. This new trend has resulted in many men's magazines flying off the shelves. There is a flourishing industry now in male health diet supplements and performance enhancing agents. Meanwhile, huge advertising budgets are being used to customise the ideal male body. Many sports men and actors are being used as the clotheshorses for this new phenomenon in society. Unfortunately, there is little associated information in respect to the damage and dangers associated with anabolic steroid use and the significant long term damage of the abuse of these agents.

Chapter 8
Human Growth hormone

"Nothing goes to sleep as easily as one's conscience"
Anon

What is HGH?
Human Growth Hormone (HGH) is a naturally occurring hormone in a healthy human body. HGH is produced by the pituitary gland situated deep in the middle of the brain. It is responsible for proper growth and development in all humans. Normal growth in children is dependent on the proper secretion of HGH and once adulthood is reached it plays an important role in metabolism.

HGH is responsible for a person growing taller, but there are other areas where HGH helps in human development. HGH is proven to reverse muscle wasting in persons suffering from AIDS. It is claimed that HGH supplements slow down the ageing process making one live longer. Many advertisements are run on American TV boasting the benefits of HGH to the aging male and female. Claims of increased sexual potency to greater elasticity of the skin are made. None of these claims has been proven.

Growth hormone abuse in sport
Growth hormone (GH), growth hormone releasing factor (GHRF), and related somatotrophins are prohibited by both the International Olympic Committee and the National Collegiate Athletic Association in the United States of America. They are categorized as peptide hormones. In the nineteen eighties, human growth hormone became more readily available for children with a growth hormone deficiency and short stature, following the advances in synthetic production via recombinant DNA cloning. Abuse among athletes is thought to occur due to its lipolytic effect. There has been no evidence of increased skeletal muscle mass or strength in non-deficiency states; however, the effect on body fat appears to be sufficient for the abuse of this drug. There are many side effects

associated with the abuse of human growth hormone, including gigantism and acromegaly, as well as the associated metabolic and endocrine disorders.

The control of Human Growth Hormone (GH) release is complex.

GH is released from the pituitary gland at the base of the brain.Its release is under the control of 2 Hypothalamic hormones(a higher control centre in the brain: One which inhibits release :SST; (Somatostatin), and the other which stimulates secretion GHRH (Somatocrenin)

Other agents and situations (neurotransmitters, drugs, insulin, hormones, stress, sleep, hypoglycaemia) can all influence the release of Growth Hormone

Human Growth Hormone stimulates the release of 2 peptide hormones :insulin like growth factor type 1(IGF 1), and insulin like growth factor 2(IGF 2) from the liver. Both growth hormone and the IGF`s have an effect on muscle growth, by promoting amino acid uptake , and stimulation of protein synthesis

Growth Hormone Axis

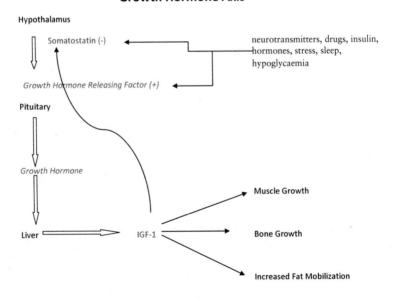

GH actions are complex , and effect organs and cells, in a bi-phasic manner.

In the acute phase GH alone stimulates amino uptake into muscles and the liver, thus promoting muscle growth. There is increased glucose uptake into the muscles and fat cells and fat metabolism reduces.

In the chronic phase the IGFs cause an increase in fatty acid breakdown, an increase in fat metabolism and a reduction in glucose metabolism resulting in fat loss.

GH is frequently taken in conjunction with Anabolic steroids and IGFs, by an abusing individual, as it is considered to have a synergistic effect and is more affective in increasing lean body mass and reducing visceral fat mass.

There is also the suggestion that long-term abuse may be associated with leukaemia. Infection is also a problem with the abuse of human growth hormone. In the illicit market, much of the human growth hormone is derived from cadavers, and may be contaminated by viruses such as the AIDS virus and Creutzfeldt-Jakob disease (CJD).

HGH History
Researcher's first attempt at treating growth hormone deficiency was to purify bovine growth hormone (rBGH) for use in GH-deficient humans. Since the nineteen twenties, doctors have been using a purified form of bovine insulin to treat insulin dependent Type 1 Diabetes Mellitus. However, bovine growth hormone has a different molecular structure than human growth hormone, so this treatment was ultimately unsuccessful.

The first successful human treatment of growth hormone deficiency was in 1958. Maurice Raben, an endocrinologist at Tufts University School of Medicine in Boston, Massachusetts, was able to purify enough GH from the pituitary glands of an autopsied body to treat GH-deficiency in a seventeen year-old boy.

After hearing of Raben's successful treatment, many endocrinologists began to make arrangements with local morgues in order to obtain the pituitary glands of autopsied cadavers. This form of growth hormone became known as cadaver-GH.

In 1960, the U.S. National Institutes of Health formed a branch called the National Pituitary Agency in order to better control the procurement and distribution of cadaver-GH. The National Pituitary Agency arranged for large scale procurement and purification of cadaver-GH and distributed it to select endocrinologists for the treatment of GH-deficiency in children. Several other countries followed by developing their own cadaver-GH controlling agencies.

Treatment for GH-deficiency in this manner was reserved for only the most severe cases. Only children who suffered from GH-deficiency were allowed treatment, and treatment ceased when a child reached a minimal height. For these reasons, few children were treated during the twenty years of cadaver-GH treatment.

In the late 1970s, Swedish pharmaceutical company, Kabi, began to contract the purchase of pituitary glands from European hospitals for the first commercial GH product, Crescormon. Kabi advertised Crescormon with the slogan 'Now you determine the need' working off of the idea that treatment, until then, had been limited by government controlled agencies.

In 1985, four cases of CJD were diagnosed in patients who had been treated with cadaver-GH in the nineteen sixties. By 2003, that number had risen to twenty-six. The use of cadaver-GH quickly ceased upon the discovery of the similar GH treatments that each CJD-diagnosed individual received in their youth.

However, in 1981, American pharmaceutical company, Genentech, after collaborating with Kabi, developed the first synthetic human growth hormone. Known as recombinant human growth hormone (rhGH), this form of synthetic GH was produced using a biosynthetic process called Inclusion Body Technology. Human growth hormone produced by Inclusion Body Technology became known as Somatrem. Later, an improved process of creating rhGH was developed called Protein Secretion technology. This method is the most common form of current HGH synthesis; it is known as Somatropin.

Effects of Growth Hormone

The most common side effects seen during a study on GH therapy were; arthralgias and edema, probably reflecting the pharmacologic dose of GH used and the resultant supraphysiologic levels of IGF-I.

Significant hyperglycemia and frank diabetes mellitus can be precipitated by GH therapy.

How is HGH made?

Up to a decade ago HGH was made by removing the pituitary gland from dead bodies and processing it. The processed hormones were injected into HGH deficient persons. The illegal market in HGH used a similar source for the raw material production of HGH with cadaver pituitary glands spun down to a powdered form before they were packaged into pills for human consumption. The problem with this method of production was an incomplete kill of any bacteria in the cadaver's pituitary gland, resulting in an infected batch of HGH. There have been a number of anecdotal reports in the literature citing this cause for individuals contracting HIV; Hepatitis B and Mad Cow Disease. Currently HGH is made via genetic engineering which is a complex procedure, which carries little or no risk of infection.

HGH uses

HGH today need not be given by your doctor as an injection. It is available as pills and nasal sprays.

HGH is helpful for children with HGH deficiency. This deficiency keeps their growth stunted. HGH supplements help them grow normally. This treatment will not be of any use to a stunted child who has got a normal secretion of HGH, but is stunted due to some other reason.

Many athletes have taken to using HGH for its claimed muscle building and stamina increasing properties.

The use of HGH has increased of late since advertisers make you believe that HGH is the magic potion that can cure a vast variety of ailments. In 1992, 5% of an adolescent sporting population admitted experimenting with GH. In 1997, 12.7% of gym based steroid abusers also co-abused GH. In the early 1990's IGF-1 emerged on the "black market" in the USA, and had spread to Europe by the mid 1990's.UK research has shown that 14% of male bodybuilders had used IGF. Many fall for these false and unproven claims and take HGH without any medical consultation. It is very possible that such people will suffer from some side effects, thus, not benefiting at all.

HGH Side Effects Profile

As growth hormone is naturally produced in the human body, the side effects of HGH treatment are rare. Generally, these side effects are caused by taking higher than recommended doses of HGH over longer than recommended periods of time. However, HGH has been known to occasionally cause:

Hypoglycemia

Hypoglycemia is a medical emergency associated with low blood sugar. It can produce a variety of symptoms and effects but the principal problems arise from an inadequate supply of glucose to the brain, resulting in impairment of function Effects can range from vaguely "feeling bad" to seizures, unconsciousness, and occasionally permanent brain damage or death.

In people with diabetes, their bodies do not produce an adequate amount of insulin, leading to dangerously high glucose levels. People with hypoglycemia have too much insulin, leading to too low glucose levels. Because HGH increases the level of insulin in your body, some people have suffered from hypoglycemia after taking HGH drugs.

Ancromeglia
Acromeglia is a disease that causes abnormal bone growth. HGH cannot cause acromeglia, but it can speed up the progression of the disease in people predisposed to it.

Carpal Tunnel Syndrome
Carpal tunnel syndrome is caused by a pinched nerve in the wrist. It can lead to loss of hand movement. HGH has been known to cause carpal tunnel syndrome in users who do not take the drug as directed.

HGH from reputed manufacturers is safe if used under proper supervision, but it comes with a small disadvantage; it is expensive. Many who take HGH without supervision buy spurious products that come at a lower price. The side effects of indiscriminate use of HGH are bad, and it just gets worse when counterfeit products are used. Persons who share needles to inject themselves with HGH are at a high risk of transmission of blood-borne viruses (the deadliest and most common being the AIDS virus).

Some of the known side effects of the undue use of HGH are listed as follows:
• Acromegaly (as described in detail below)

- Premature death (in case of acromegaly)
- Heart enlargement (due to prolonged use of HGH; cannot be reversed)
- Low blood sugar with risk of going into a diabetic coma
- Excessive hair growth all over the body
- Excessive water retention
- Liver damage
- Thyroid damage

The most common side effect of the excess use of HGH is acromegaly. This is a medical condition that begins with the overgrowth of facial bone and connective tissue, leading to a changed appearance due to protruding jaw and eyebrow bones. This condition also leads to an abnormal growth of the hands and feet with an increased growth of hair all over the body. Contrary to increasing your life, this condition will shorten life expectancy considerably.

Cost of GH and IGF

GH and IGF are both expensive in the black market. GH cost aproximately€650 per month for a course of 2 IU/day. IGF-1 is also expensive at €900 per milligram, with up to one and a half milligrams being used by abusers monthly, at doses ranging from 30 to 50 micrograms a day. These once expensive niche drugs costing thousands of pounds a dose, have now become more common in high street gyms across Europe, and have become a drug of choice for body image abusers. In 2007, Sylvester Stallone was ordered to pay £5,400 in fines and costs by a court in Australia for possession of growth hormone. In 2010 the Canadian celebrity doctor, Anthony Galea, was charged with possession of growth hormone and administering it to clients. The drug is not banned in all sports, despite pressure from sports legislators. In August 2012 the National Football league of America(NFL) Players' Union agreed to start checking for human growth hormone. However in December 2012 there were still arguments in

Congress that the league will head into next season without a test for the banned drug.

Despite the evidence that drugs such as GH and IGF are dangerous to health, there is still a reluctance to put the athlete's well being ahead of commercial gain.

Beware of Beneficial Claims of HGH Made by Quacks

Many HGH marketers will make you believe that HGH can solve a variety of human deficiencies. They claim that taking HGH supplements will strengthen your immune system, grow thick hair on a bald head, build muscle fast making you look like a bodybuilder, increase your stamina and improve your sex life, improve your memory like never before, improve your vision to perfection, burn down fat without exercising or giving up your favourite junk foods; this list can just go on and on. If all these claims were true, there would be no illnesses, everyone would have the perfect body without doing anything and we would all be living in a world where nothing could be made more perfect. All these claims are usually made to sell HGH supplements that are very expensive and would not sell otherwise.

Chapter 9

ERYTHROPOIETIN

"I have nothing to offer but blood, toil sweat and tears"
Winston Churchill

What is erythropoietin?

Erythropoietin (EPO) is a hormone produced by the kidney that promotes the formation of red blood cells in the bone marrow. EPO is a glycoprotein (a protein with a sugar attached to it). Human EPO has a molecular weight of thirty-four thousand. The kidney cells that make EPO are specialized and are sensitive to low oxygen levels in the blood. These cells release EPO when the oxygen level is low in the kidney. EPO then stimulates the bone marrow to produce more red cells and thereby increases the oxygen-carrying capacity of the blood.

EPO is the prime regulator of red blood cell production. Its major functions are to promote the differentiation and development of red blood cells and to initiate the production of hemoglobin, the molecule within red cells that transports oxygen.

The EPO gene has been found on human chromosome 7. EPO is produced not only in the kidney but also, to a lesser extent, in the liver. Different DNA sequences flanking the EPO gene act to control kidney versus liver production of EPO.

Synthetic Erythropoietin Production

Using recombinant DNA technology, EPO has been synthetically produced for use in persons with certain types of anaemia, such as anemia due to kidney failure, anemia secondary to AZT treatment of AIDS, anemia associated with cancer, and anemia associated with chronic disease.

Erythropoietin and blood doping are an effort to improve aerobic function.

The maximum oxygen uptake is the amount of oxygen per kilogram per min that can be delivered by an exercising muscle. The ability to deliver this oxygen referred to as the VO2 max, (the maximal oxygen uptake) is limited by a number of physiological components, namely the cardiac output and the oxygen carrying capacity of the blood.

The cardiac output in highly trained athletes is usually at a maximal or close to maximal level insuring that a large amount of blood is transmitted per heart beat throughout the body. The oxygen carrying capacity is determined by the total body haemoglobin.

The haemoglobin carries oxygen to the exercising cells. It is not possible to artificially increase the hemoglobin content of individual red blood cells hence, the strategy to improve this element of aerobic performance is to increase the number of red blood cells and hence, the overall quantity of the haemoglobin that is and thus the amount of oxygen than can be delivered to the exercising muscles.

Altitude training
Altitude training is a physiological adaptive strategy used by many athletes. By exercising or ascending to altitude, the body physiologically increases its red cell mass and in turn its ability to carry oxygen. This effect, however, can be short-lived and comes with other side-effects such as headache, nausea and irritability and it may take up to twelve weeks at altitude to have a significant effect on athletic performance.

Blood doping
In the 1970s and early 1980s, subjects own packed red blood cells were used and re-infused into the subject. This effect however was also very short-lived and also carries significant hazards for the individual engaged in this type of blood doping. Blood doping is a method of increasing the number of red blood cells in the body which in turn carry more oxygen to the muscles. It is most often used by athletes who compete in high endurance races like cycling or cross-country skiing.

Blood doping involves removing a litre of blood from an athlete's system and then freezing and storing it for several weeks. A day or two before a big race, the stored blood would then be re-injected into the athlete's system - creating extra red blood cells. These extra red blood cells would carry more oxygen to the muscles - giving the athlete an advantage over the other racers who don't use blood doping.

Erythropoietin
In 1985, synthetic erythropoietin became available through specialized recombinant DNA technology. Recombinant erythropoietin was invented for the stimulation of erythropoiesis. This was used by renal patients and also by individuals with debilitating diseases which resulted in chronic anaemia.

Erythropoietin stimulates red blood cell production. With more red blood cells, athletes are able to carry more oxygen in their blood and enhance endurance exercise ability.

Recombinant erythropoietin and other variations of erythropoietin were abused by the athletic population from the initial discovery of the compound. Within months of the advent of this agent, a number of endurance athletes died from a combination of stroke and cardiovascular episodes. Additional dangers of EPO include sudden death during sleep, which has killed approximately eighteen pro-cyclists since the 1980s.

These athletes included some cyclists (in the Tour de France), long-distance runners, speed skaters, and Nordic (cross-country) skiers. On the last day of the 2002 Winter Olympics in Salt Lake City, three cross-country skiers were evicted from the Games for blood doping. Two of the skiers lost their medals; the other was disqualified from the games. The version of EPO supposedly used by the skiers in Salt Lake City is called darbepoetin.

The sudden use of erythropoietin resulted in an elevation of the viscosity of the blood. The blood in many instances became sludge-like and normal transmission through the blood vessels became difficult. This resulted in end-organ death, resulting in cardiac events such as heart attack and brain vascular events such as strokes.

9 orienteering athletes died from heart attacks and strokes in the late 1980s, months after EPO was launched as a medical agent. EPO was considered to be a causative factor in these athletes' unnecessary deaths.

There are a number of variations of erythropoietin which are used in normal medical practice. In the case of normal medical practice, regular blood testing and monitoring of the haematocrit (the viscosity of the blood) is undertaken and careful adherence to the correct dosage of this very powerful agent is also undertaken by practicing physicians.

In the case of those who abuse this agent, if they are not being adequately supervised, this very powerful drug can very quickly result in extreme elevation in the red blood cell count and haematocrit, resulting in a significant increase in viscosity with catastrophic endpoints such as a heart attack, stroke and death.

Plasma Expanders
Plasma expanders may be used to mask the raised haematocrit (viscosity) caused by erythropoietin. This is a banned method under the WADA rules. One such agent is hydroxyethyl starch, which results in the plasma volume of the blood being expanded over a twenty-hour period. This drug will ensure that the viscosity of the blood does not rise to a critical level. The use of these plasma expanders has resulted in many side effects. The abuse of this agent while not ensuring an enhancement of performance will mask the effect of erythropoietin and therefore is also a banned substance.

Actovegin

Actovegin is also considered to be a form of blood doping. Actovegin is a derivative of calf blood and contains a number of substances (nucleic acid, peptides and oligosaccharides). Actovegin has been shown to improve glucose tolerance in diabetic patients. Actovegin was initially considered in the year 2000 to be an oxygen carrying agent however, some months later, the medical commission of the Olympic movement announced that it is unclear about the mode of action of the drug and if in fact this drug enhances performance. It has also been used to reduce pain and has a significant anti-inflammatory effect. Nevertheless, Actovegin is on the prohibited list under the WADA rules.

Erythropoietin and disease

The measurement of EPO in the blood is useful in the study of bone marrow disorders and kidney disease. Normal levels of EPO are 0-19 mU/ml (milliunits per milliliter). Elevated levels of EPO can be seen in Polycythemia, a disorder in which there is an excess of red blood cells. The sufferer usually presents with a ruddy complexion complaining of breathlessness.

Lower than normal levels of EPO are seen in chronic renal failure, chronic systemic diseases and in HIV patients.

Abnormal EPO levels have also been noted in infants who have died from Sudden Infant Death Syndrome (SIDS). The French researcher at Rouen University has shown an association between Sudden Infant Death and high levels of erythropoietin. The normal values were low at birth and progressively increased during the first two years. In the sudden infant death (SID) group the EPO level was significantly higher in comparison to a normal population.

Therefore the non supervised use and abuse of EPO in a non-athletic setting is potentially very dangerous and will interfere with normal blood function, and health.

Side effects associated with EPO use

EPO has been used in clinical practice for over twenty years. There are well recognised side effects which occur even in a supervised medical setting.

Already hypertensive patients may experience further elevation of blood pressure, and a minority of patients (perhaps 20-30%) with chronic renal failure may experience increased blood pressure, when given intravenous EPO. This is thought to be caused by the rapid increase in hematocrit. For the same reason, some patients may develop blood clots. These undesirable reactions are less common when the drug is administered subcutaneously.

Recently Eprex, a commercial form of EPO has been associated with incidences of pure red-cell aplasia, a condition which, though rare, can lead to permanent blood transfusion dependency.

Possible minor side effects include: diarrhoea, dizziness, headache, itching, muscle aches and pains, nausea, pain at the site of injection, tiredness, or vomiting. These side effects usually diminish or disappear as the body adjusts to the medication.

Dangers with EPO abuse in sport

When misused during athletic activity, EPO is thought to be especially dangerous. This is because dehydration can further increase the viscosity of the blood, increasing the risk of heart attacks and strokes. The mechanism of death due to EPO is thought to be increased hematocrit (red blood cells).

The erythropoietin will increase the hematocrit to high levels in any endurance event. Dehydration will push the hematocrit even higher, causing clotting in the blood vessels to the brain or to the heart. These clots interrupt normal blood flow to the end organ (heart, brain liver and spleen) resulting in an 'infarction' or local cell death which often results in that organ failing and death.

Detection of Erythropoietin abuse

Erythropoietin is a banned substance in the WADA code of substances. It is banned as a blood doping offence, and is included in the banned substance list under this category. Its detection in an athlete usually results in a ban from the sport of two to four years. There are a number of confirmatory procedures to detect this practice.

Blood testing of Haemtocrit

When WADA and the International Olympic Committee banned EPO, the routine screening of haematocrit was suggested as a way of detecting an abuser. However, defining an appropriate cut-off level for hameatocrit is a fundamental problem. Haematocrit levels greater than 0.52 in an otherwise healthy individual in the absence of a renal tumour or polycythaemia rubra vera would suggest an abuser. Recombinant ertytroprotein (rEPO) is identical to natural EPO immunologically and biologically, and is almost identical structurally. rEPO effects far outlast its detectability, and rEPO levels in the blood can return to baseline within days of injection. Routine haematocrit testing may be used as a screening method; however, it is not foolproof, and does not give specific proof of abuse of EPO.

Recombinant erythropoietin (rEPO) has a short half-life of approximately four to six hours when administered intravenously, and the detection of erythropoietin administration by determining abnormal concentrations in blood or urine is therefore difficult as the abuser can take steps to avoid giving a sample following administration of the drug. Detection of this substance has always proved to be difficult. In the past few years this status has radically changed.

Isoelectric pattern of Erythropoietin

The detection in urine of recombinant human erythropoietin (rEPO), a hormone misused by endurance athletes as a doping agent, is based on the differentiation of its isoelectric pattern from that of the corresponding natural hormone. Different profiles of the isoelectric pattern exist for synthetic rEPO and the naturally occurring EPO which the body naturally produces. Hence an abuser is detected by the presence of rogue EPO which has a different electrical pattern to that which he or she naturally produces. Research has concluded that this method of EPO abuse is accurate and shows no false positives. This methodology of detection was introduced at the Olympic Games in Sydney, and many positive tests followed.

Erythropoitein abuse in professional bike-riders
EPO has been particularly abused among the cycling community. Over eighteen professional riders' deaths from 1990 are associated with the abuse of this agent eg: Phillip Gaumont, who admitted EPO use during a 2003 tour. In 2005 he wrote a book, *Prisonnier du Dopage* ('Prisoner of doping') describing doping methods, masking methods and financial pressures. He implicated David Millar who later confessed to EPO use after police found traces in his hotel room. Others include those listed below:

- 2004 **David Millar** confesses to EPO use after traces found in flat. Banned for two years.
- 2005 **Dario Frigo** expelled from 2005 Tour de France after products found in car.
- 2005 **Roberto Heras** won a forth consecutive Vuelta a Espagne but tested positive for EPO and was stripped of title.
- 2007 **Alexandre Vinokourov** failed test for blood doping after winning time trial during Tour de France.
- 2007 **Michael Rasmussen.** Whilst wearing the yellow jersey, Rasmussen was sacked by his team Rabobank for lying about his whereabouts in the previous months. Rasmussen was actually in Mexico and unable to take dope tests.
- 2007 **Iban Mayo** tested positive for EPO to take the anti-doping tests.
- 2008 **Manuel Beltran** positive for EPO in Tour De France

- **2008 Riccardo Ricci** positive for EPO after winning mountain top stage in Tour De France. Ricci later admitted to taking EPO on ten previous stages and admitted tests failed to pick up many occasions of EPO use.

Conclusion

EPO is a widely available drug. It has significant effects and side effects. It has been of great clinical assistance to those suffering from chronic anaemias associated with specific diseases. It also has been shown to improve endurance performance by increasing the oxygen carrying capacity of blood. It however, has a significant serious side effect profile. The medical literature is littered with anecdotal examples of individuals who have died from its abuse. Death usually results from an unnatural increased viscosity of the blood which prevents normal blood flow to vital organs such as the heart and brain; resulting in heart attack and/or stroke. This potential is greatly increased in individuals who are taking exercise, as the dehydration associated with sporting activity and exercise will cause further increases in blood viscosity resulting in 'sludgy' blood and catastrophe.

Chapter 10
ALCOHOL

"Long quaffing maketh a short life"
John Lyly

Since earliest times the use of alcohol among the athletic and exercising population has been well documented. The ancient Greeks fermented berries in an effort to improve exercise performance. They considered fermented berries to be an elixir. In more recent times it has been shown that the use of alcohol in the acute setting (that is before you take exercise) has an extremely hazardous effect on exercise performance. Alcohol acts as a diuretic and this can result in dehydration and poor exercise performance.

Incidence of Alcohol use among the sporting population
Alcohol and sport have been linked since ancient times, when alcohol was considered to be the elixir of life. Alcohol is the most widely used drug among the athletic population. It has been reported that up to 88% of intercollegiate American athletes use alcohol.

This is similar to the normal adult consumption of alcohol in North America, where 90% of the population consumes this beverage. Different sports appear to have different drinking patterns. In an Irish survey, traditional field sports such as rugby, cricket, hurling, soccer and Gaelic football were found to have the highest percentage of athletes who consume alcohol compared with sports such as horse racing, cycling and tennis.

Social and Physical Considerations
Up to 90% of the adult population drinks alcohol. It is therefore often difficult to define 'problem drinking'. The World Health Organization defines alcoholism as 'drinking that cause's emotional, social or physical damage to the individual'. It is

equally well described in 1985 as 'a social disorder with medical complications'. Young men (18 to 24 years old) have been shown to have an increased chance of problem drinking.

Sports clubs are often the places where young people are exposed to alcohol and socialise independently of their family and guardians. Athletes and officials are no different from the general public when it comes to problem drinking. In fact, those involved in sport may be at a greater risk of alcohol-related problems as the opportunity to drink is often present in the sport pavilion. Athletes who have to retire early due to injury have also been shown to run the risk of alcohol-related problems. Research has also shown that intercollegiate athletes had a significantly higher proportion of 'risky' lifestyle behaviour patterns compared with nonathletes. These include increased alcohol consumption, driving while intoxicated and riding in a car with an intoxicated driver. Therefore, it is important that sporting clubs advise on patterns of alcohol consumption amongst its athletes.

Alcohol, the Law and Education
Over the past decades there have been many instances of high profile sporting athletes who have run into significant problems with alcohol, and many sports stars have also served custodial sentences for drink driving offences.

In North America, the use and abuse of alcohol is considered to be the most pervasive drug problem on college campus. It is a particular priority of the National Collegiate Athletic Association (NCAA), which has a number of prevention and education programmes designed to address this issue. One of these is the NCAA/Betty Ford Center Alcoholism and Drug Addiction Awareness Program. The program educates university officials and coaches on alcoholism and drug addiction. This gives the coach, who is the first person likely to identify a problem, an understanding of the warning signs of an alcohol abuser.

Sports administrators should familiarize themselves with methods of identification and detection of alcohol abusers. The CAGE questionnaire can be used to do this. It is a simple 4-question self-test which may help you become aware of your use or abuse of alcohol. This test specifically focuses on alcohol use, and not on the use of other drugs. This is a worthwhile public health intervention, and is frequently used in North American College sports teams.

The Effects of Alcohol on Sports Performance

Many recreational athletes still believe that short term ingestion of small amounts of alcohol enhances athletic performance. In 1982, the American College of Sports Medicine[1] conducted a comprehensive analysis related to the effects of alcohol on human physical performance and came to the following conclusions:

- *The acute* ingestion of alcohol has a deleterious effect on many psychomotor skills.

- Alcohol consumption does not substantially influence physiological function crucial to physical performance, maximal oxygen uptake, respiratory dynamics and cardiac function.

- *Alcohol will not improve muscular work capacity and may decrease performance levels.*

- Alcohol may impair temperature regulation during prolonged exercise in a cold environment. More recent research suggests that the acute ingestion of alcohol does in fact decrease performance levels.

In 1983, research found that total cycling time to exhaustion was always shorter after alcohol use than after placebo. In 1985, a study on 10 athletes showed that serum alcohol concentrations over 100 mg/dl weaken the pumping force of the heart, even in healthy young adults.

In 1987, a study of 18 male runners who underwent a 5-mile treadmill run showed that the average running time was 28 seconds longer after alcohol consumption.

These findings imply that the acute ingestion of alcohol before exercise should be actively discouraged as it adversely affects athletic performance. This practice frequently continues at a recreational level in traditional sports such as rugby and soccer.

Alcohol Metabolism

85-95% of alcohol is metabolized in the liver by the enzyme alcohol dehydrogenase, and this occurs at the relatively slow fixed rate of 100 mg/kg per hour. This equates to a metabolic rate of 10 g per hour for a 100 kg man. There is a significant variation from person to person in the rate at which they metabolize alcohol.

Exercise will not increase alcohol metabolism. Many recreational athletes believe that short-term ingestion of small amounts of alcohol enhances athletic performance.

The American College of Sports Medicine conducted a comprehensive analysis of the science relating to the acute effects of alcohol in human performance in 1982. This showed that while the acute ingestion of alcohol had a deleterious effect on many cycle motor skills, it did not substantially influence physiological functions crucial to physical performance (VO2 max, respiratory dynamics and cardiac function).

The Hangover effect of Alcohol
The majority of individuals who will drink the evening before participation are subject to the hangover effect of alcohol during their exercise and activity. Research that was conducted in Dublin and London has indicated that the hangover effect of alcohol has a significantly deleterious effect on aerobic performance and function.

The delayed effects of alcohol have also been considered, and it is suggested that a hangover will reduce aerobic performance due to its dehydrating effect on available carbohydrate and its effect on blood lactate levels.

The Effect of Alcohol on Aerobic Metabolism
The enzyme alcohol dehydrogenase metabolises the majority of alcohol in the liver, which occurs at the relatively slow fixed rate of 100 mg/kg/h.

This equates to a metabolic rate of 10 g/h for a 100kg athlete. Therefore, it will take up to 10 hours to metabolise 10 g of alcohol: hence, only-limited amounts can be disposed of in any period of time. Rates will be even slower for smaller athletes. Exercise will not increase alcohol metabolism. Alcohol metabolism affects certain chemical processes in the body reducing aerobic function.

1. Effect on the Citric Acid Cycle
Alcohol is oxidised in hepatic cytosal by alcohol dehydrogenase. This reaction leads to an accumulation of free NADH and an increase in the NADH: NAD ratio. This reduction in NAD causes a slowing in the citric acid cycle at the inalate de-hydrogenasc step (which is NAD dependent), resulting in a slowing of aerobic metabolism.

2. Effect on the Lactate : Pyruvate Ratio
85% of alcohol is metabolized in the liver by the enzyme Alcohol dehydorgenase.

As the alcohol is being metabolized to aledhyde the substrate NAD takes up a hydrogen ion (H+) resulting in an increase in the chemical substrate NADH.

This increases the NADH to NAD ratio, which increases the production of lactic acid from pyruvate, increasing the lactate to pyruvate ratio.

Increased levels of lactic acid will then limit activity during strenuous exercise, as further lactic acid is produced during exercise. The body's ability to mop up this acid by the buffering system is over loaded resulting in a higher circulating lactic acid level. This will reduce aerobic function, and cause a reduction in the body's physiological performance.

3. Dehydrating Effect
Alcohol causes dehydration. Dehydration of the order of 2% of the body weight can reduce aerobic function by 10%; which also has a significant impact in aerobic physiological function.

4. Effect on Available Carbohydrate
Skeletal muscle functions most efficiently aerobically when it uses carbohydrate as its primary fuel. It has been reported that alcohol ingestion will lower muscle glycogen levels. It is also suggested that there is a decrease in spleen's ability to release glucose associated with alcohol intake. The NADH produced by the alcohol dehydrogenase reaction inhibits gluconeogenesis, (release of glucose into the blood and tissues) with a resultant reduction in blood sugar. These factors will decrease the available fuel for normal aerobic energy production.

5. Psychological Effect
Alcohol hangover is caused by alcohol toxicity, dehydration and the toxic effects of the congeners in alcoholic drinks. It is commonly characterised by a depressed mood, headache and hypersensitivity to outside stimuli. As a result, the athlete may not feel able to perform maximally.

Beer the beverage of choice for Sportsmen and Women

Beer is the choice of the majority of athletes who drink alcohol. A 330ml (12oz) can of beer contains approximately one-hundred and fifty calories and, of this, only fifty calories are in the form of carbohydrate. It is recommended that athletes consume two hundred and four hundred calories of carbohydrate within two hours of exercise, and then repeat these two hours later. To achieve this with one beer alone, the athlete would have to drink up to eight cans of beer. This is both impractical and unwise, especially when a pint of fruit juice would meet the carbohydrate requirements. Beer is not therefore recommended as a fluid or nutritional replacement for the exercising athlete.

Alcohol is the drug most used by the athletic population. In general, 85-90% of all athletes drink alcohol, and certain sports such as rugby union football traditionally have a higher incidence of alcohol use among players.

Dangers of alcohol in Sport

The acute use of alcohol in the sports setting is associated with much morbidity and mortality. In particular, alcohol use on the water (either recreational or competitive) is significantly associated with drowning and near drowning episodes, and alcohol is a contributory factor in at least 60% of all boating fatalities.

A large proportion of those injured on the water have blood alcohol concentrations at a level that would preclude them from driving a motor vehicle.

The acute use of alcohol has also been shown to reduce hand-eye coordination, and therefore operating a mechanically propelled vehicle or performing a high speed or motor activity requiring skill while under the influence of alcohol may increase the chances of an accident.

Alcohol ingestion may also cause abnormal cardiac rhythms. This pro-arrhythmogenic in susceptible individuals can be a causative factor for supraventricular tachycardias and atrial fibrillation. Its effect on the myocardium is ergolytic in that it decreases the pumping properties of the myocardium. Alcohol is also associated with an increased incidence of upper respiratory tract infections in running athletes.

The use of alcohol while performing more high-speed activities such as equestrian activities and nautical activities has been shown to be a significant causative effect in injury and occasional mortality.

Alcohol a banned substance
Alcohol is subject to certain restrictions in competitive sports. It is a prohibited substance in some aiming events due to its ability to reduce tremors. Blood or breath alcohol levels may be requested in fencing and shooting events in the modern pentathlon; therefore, athletes competing in these events are advised to abstain from alcoholic beverages for at least twelve hours before the event.

Alcohol and injury incidence
Research has also indicated that individuals who drink alcohol the evening before participation in exercise or physical activity are two times more likely to suffer injury while they are participating in the sport or activity. During normal alcohol consumption the body produces excess amounts of lactic acid.

When one starts to exercise within the following twenty-four or thirty-six hours, greater levels of lactic acid than expected accumulate. The body's normal buffering system cannot mop up the access lactic acid. This results in increased muscle fatigue, and a greater level of intrinsic muscle tears and injury.

Previous research has indicated that the consumption of alcohol in the 24 hours prior to athletic activity significantly alters aerobic performance. This reduction of aerobic performance is reported to be of the order of 11 %.

Recent research has shown that there is a significant difference in injury rates between drinkers and nondrinkers in the athletic population. Those athletes who consumed alcohol at least once per week had a much higher injury rate, more than double that of athletes who were non-drinkers.

Conclusion
Alcohol is a beverage widely used by many recreational and competitive athletes. The actual quantity consumed by the serious athlete is quite low. Those involved in sport are more likely to be exposed to alcohol due to the social nature of many sporting clubs.

Alcohol is a very poor rehydrating fluid for athletes who have been engaged in strenuous activity. It has also been shown to have no positive effects on athletic performance and is a significant aetiological factor in sports participation morbidity and mortality. The effect of alcohol ingestion on the day before activity is set to cause a significant decrease in aerobic performance. It is also now known that sportsmen and women who drink alcohol one or more times a week have twice the injury rate of nondrinkers.

Education of athletes to the possible harmful effects of alcohol is essential. Therefore, it is incumbent on those associated with sport to disseminate the information regarding the harmful effects of alcohol on human physical performance.

Chapter 11

HYDRATION

"If you can lead it to water, and force it to drink, it isn't a horse"
Anon

Hydration is one of the most important factors in physiological performance. Adequate hydration is essential for normal physiological and muscle contraction and function.

Dehydration is one of the bugbears of all those who take exercise. Very few of us are adequately hydrated when we perform activities and indeed dehydrating is much more common than we previously thought. In the equestrian world no horse would ever be allowed on the gallops unless it was adequately hydrated because horse trainers are very aware of the significant impact dehydration has on equine function.

Dehydration is the relative absence or reduction in intracellular fluid. Dehydration has a number of physiological consequences; fatigue, loss of concentration, headache, muscle cramps and a reduction in aerobic performance.

Dehydration of 2% of the body weight can reduce aerobic (endurance) performance by 20% or more. This has a significant effect on all athletic performance and on the occurrence of injury. It also has a significant impact on day to day cognitive function and daily work and social abilities. In simple terms dehydrated individuals get injured and do not perform to the best of their abilities.

Clinical research has also confirmed this, and in a recent state consensus of the British Journal of Sports Medicine, it suggested that loss of fluid and reduction of body carbohydrates stores are the two major causes of fatigue in prolonged exercise.

In an average individual 55% of your body consists of water. This water plays a critical role in many processes of the body and all of us should drink at least two litres of fluid everyday to keep our bodies fully hydrated. For those who perform regular exercise, fluid intake should become even more important. During exercise body temperature increases and we start to sweat. For this reason water intake needs to be increased to replace the addition fluid lost as sweat.

Sweating is the way in which the body maintains its core temperature at thirty-seven degrees centigrade. There is also loss of body fluids and electrolytes (minerals such as chloride, calcium, magnesium, sodium and potassium) and if unchecked will lead to dehydration and eventually to medical conditions, the worst of which is a condition referred to as heat stroke.

Bodily functions and physiology alters as we lose a percentage of body weight in perspiration.

Percentage of body weight lost as sweat	Physiological effect
2% body weight lost as sweat	Impaired performance
4% body weight lost as sweat	Capacity for most of the work declines
5% body weight lost as sweat	Heat exhaustion
7% body weight lost as sweat	Hallucinations
10% body weight lost as sweat	Circulatory collapse and heat stroke

During physical activities it is quite easy to lose at least one litre of fluid during an hour of endurance exercise. Therefore it is easy to lose 2% of your body weight through sweat during exercise.

The exact volume of sweat loss will vary depending on the type, duration and intensity of the exercise, but other levels would suggest that running or walking ten kilometres will certainly lose 2% of body weight and playing a football match would probably lose near to 3% of body weight. However, a rugby union match will also lose up to 3% and running a marathon would lose up to 6% of body weight.

How do we assess hydration?

There are many simple ways of assessing hydration and dehydration. Intracellular fluid concentration can be observed in a number of ways:

- Urine and blood analysis
- Daily body weighing
- Urine observation

Thirst is a late sign of dehydration, therefore you should not wait until you feel thirsty to rehydrate as it is too late to reverse the consequences.

In a fit and stable athlete, body weight is the most appropriate way to assess hydration. If you weigh two hundred pounds when you are fit, after exercise or during exercise if your body reduces by four pounds then you are 2% dehydrated.

Similarly, if you are a man who weighs one hundred kilograms, every kilogram lost equates to one litre of fluid that needs to be hydrated. For the majority of individuals whose body weight fluctuates, the most appropriate way is to observe your urine concentration and you should never participate in any sporting activity unless your urine is crystal clear. This is the methodology by which race horses are assessed and it is quite a reasonable way to proceed for assessing hydration in humans.

Fluids to drink for rehydration
Drinking plain water may cause bloating if done to excess. It can also suppress thirst in the short term and thus further drinking. Small regular amounts of water are therefore recommended, whilst also stimulating urine output and therefore it is inefficiently retained. Water is a poor choice when high fluid intake is required but is appropriate for low intensity activities and normal daily activities such as walking or related bicycle riding.

Water contains no carbohydrates or electrolytes and therefore it is a simple methodology of rehydration, however excessive water intake has the potential of water toxicity where the excessive water may cause dilution of blood electrolytes resulting in nausea, vomiting and occasional metabolic disturbances which can have serious consequences to muscle and cardiovascular performance. Therefore care must be taken when drinking large volumes of water.

Fluids to re-hydrate when exercising
All fluids taken during exercise should include water, electrolytes and carbohydrates.

Electrolytes
These electrolytes have three general functions:
1. Are essential minerals
2. Control of osmosis of water between the body and its extra and intravascular compartments
3. Help maintain the acid-base balance required for normal cellular activities

Carbohydrates

Carbohydrate is the main fuel for muscle contraction. It is stored and delivered as glucose and also is stored in the muscle. The normal body storage of carbohydrate in a typical seventy kilogram man is approximately ninety grams in the liver and four hundred as muscle glycogen. During hard exercise, this carbohydrate can be diffused with a rate of 2-4 g per minute. If this is sustained for two hours or more, a large fraction of the total body carbohydrate will be exhausted and if not replenished will significantly reduce performance.

It usually takes twenty-four to forty-eight hours for complete recovery of the glycogen stores. Therefore during exercise, it is important to take in fluids that contain small amounts of carbohydrate, although if the percentage is greater than 80% then the rate at which it is absorbed will be very slow. Therefore consuming carbohydrate before exercise is also important.

A cup of tea, an hour before one goes out walking may in fact be enough to get the sufficient carbohydrate for your exercise into your body. You do not need to have an expensive sports drink to combat the effects of dehydration or the potential effects of dehydration.

The simplest way of creating an appropriate sports drink can be made in your own kitchen by adding a half teaspoon of salt to three teaspoons of sugar mixed up in half a litre of water. This is a classical and simple rehydration drink which will work just as well as any of the commercially available products on the market.

Chapter 12
STIMULANTS AND STREET DRUGS

*"Poisons and medicine are oftentimes the same substances
given with different intents"*
Peter Mere Latham

Stimulants and their antagonists

Stimulants are a group of drugs which stimulate the Central
Nervous System (CNS) with an associated effect on the peripheral
nervous system, and a direct effect on the cardiovascular system
and the sympathetic nervous system.

The stimulant drugs pass from the blood into the brain via the
blood brain barrier. In the brain they can:
1. Stimulate the release of neurotransmitters
2. Reduce the breakdown of neurotransmitters.
3. Heighten the response of the nerves receptors.

The neurotransmitters which are released are:
- Dopamine
- Noradrenalin
- Serotonin
- Adenosine

These neurotransmitters can also be released in large quantities
during stressful situations, often referred to as "the fight or
flight" response. The actual effect of each stimulant varies
depending on the substance in question. Common effects
may include enhanced alertness, awareness, wakefulness,
endurance, productivity, and motivation. Increased arousal,
heart rate, and blood pressure are also reported, and there can
also be perception of a diminished requirement for food and
sleep. Many stimulants are also capable of improving mood
and relieving anxiety. These effects make them tempting for an
athlete.

Reports of stimulant abuse among the athletic population goes back to Ancient Greece in the third century BC, when ginseng and hallucinogenic mushrooms were regularly used. The stimulants caffeine, cocaine, strychnine and heroin were the athletes' drug of choice in the 19th Century. First report of Amphetamine use at the Olympics occurred in Berlin 1936, and in modern time's stimulant related death occurred in 1960, 1967 and 1968 in 3 professional cyclists.

Stimulants would include:

- Amphetamines
- Cocaine
- Ecstasy
- Nicotine
- Modafinil

Amphetamines

Amphetamines are a group of stimulant drugs. Amphetamine increases the levels of noradrenalin and dopamine in the brain by preventing the breakdown of the chemicals by a method called "reuptake inhibition" and by directly stimulating the increased release of these chemicals from storage vesicles in nerve cells.

Amphetamines and Sport

The prescription and administration of amphetamines are strictly controlled by laws. In the sports setting they are associated with increased aggression and alertness, which may be counter balanced with poor judgment, euphoria and a lack of self audit. Despite its frequent use most modern studies have failed to show any physical advantage to taking this drug, outside an increase in confidence.

The side effects are significant in the sportsman. Dependence is common, with higher doses being required in the chronic user. Increased susceptibility to heat stroke is also well documented, and there have been a number of well publicized fatalities, this thought to be due to the drugs effect of re-directing blood away from the skin, with interference with the normal sweating process. Their use can also mask injuries, resulting in exacerbation and progression of simple injuries

Amphetamines are frequently used in combination with other drugs. Specifically Anabolic steroid abusers frequently take a cocktail of drugs and amphetamines. Cocaine is reported to have been used in 5% of the abusers.

In a British study it was concluded that amphetamines and cocaine allowed the user train after work or stay awake during night shifts. This study particularly highlighted older door men, who needed to train after work to maintain their size and appearance, and hence regularly abuse amphetamines to allow them keep up this practice.

Amphetamines and WADA
There have been many athletes who have fallen foul of the Anti-Doping authorities by mistakenly consuming banned Amphetamines, which may be present in weak or trace amounts in Over the Counter remedies. A mistake with a nasal spray in the 2002 winter Olympics cost the British skater Alain Baxter a Bronze medal. Over the past 5 years the WADA rules relating to stimulants have changed significantly. Initially all stimulants were banned in and out of competition. This ensured that individuals who took cold and cough remedies were turning up positive drug tests. This was not necessarily the intention of WADA.

After much debate the rules relating to stimulants have been reduced to a manageable and appropriate level and are only banned in competition. Except imidazole and its derivatives (which are commonly used nasal decongestants). Adrenaline associated with local anaesthetic agents or by local administration (e.g. nasal or ophthalmologic) is not prohibited.

Ephedrine and methyl ephedrine is prohibited when its concentration in urine is greater than ten micrograms per millilitre. Pseudoephedrine is prohibited when its concentration in urine is greater than one hundred and fifty micrograms per millilitre.

Cocaine

Cocaine is a powerfully addictive stimulant drug. The powdered, hydrochloride salt form of cocaine can be snorted or dissolved in water and injected. Crack is cocaine that has not been neutralized by an acid to make the hydrochloride salt. This form of cocaine comes in a rock crystal that can be heated and its vapors smoked. The term 'crack' refers to the crackling sound heard when it is heated. Cocaine is a strong central nervous system stimulant that interferes with the re-absorption process of dopamine, a chemical messenger associated with pleasure and movement. The buildup of dopamine causes continuous stimulation of receiving neurons, which is associated with the euphoria commonly reported by cocaine abusers.

Health Hazards

Regardless of how cocaine is used or how frequently, a user can experience acute cardiovascular or cerebrovascular side effects such as a heart attack, or stroke, which can result in sudden death. Cocaine-related deaths are often a result of cardiac arrest or seizure followed by respiratory arrest.Physical effects of cocaine use include constricted blood vessels, dilated pupils, and increased temperature, heart rate, and blood pressure. The duration of cocaine's immediate euphoric effects, which include hyperstimulation, reduced fatigue, and mental alertness, depends on the route of administration; the faster the absorption, the more intense the high. On the other hand, the faster the absorption, the shorter the duration of action. The high from snorting may last fifteen to thirty minutes, while that from smoking may last five to ten minutes. Increased use can reduce the period of time a user feels high and increases the risk of addiction.

Some users of cocaine report feelings of restlessness, irritability, and anxiety. A tolerance to the 'high' may develop-many addicts' report that they seek but fail to achieve as much pleasure as they did from their first exposure. Some users will increase their doses to intensify and prolong the euphoric effects. While tolerance to the high can occur, users can also become more sensitive to cocaine's anesthetic and convulsive effects without increasing the dose taken. This increased sensitivity may explain some deaths occurring after apparently low doses of cocaine.

Use of cocaine in a binge, during which the drug is taken repeatedly and at increasingly high doses, may lead to a state of increasing irritability, restlessness, and paranoia. This can result in a period of full-blown paranoid psychosis, in which the user loses touch with reality and experiences auditory hallucinations.

Other complications associated with cocaine use include disturbances in heart rhythm and heart attacks, chest pain and respiratory failure, strokes, seizures and headaches, and gastrointestinal complications such as abdominal pain and nausea. Because cocaine has a tendency to decrease appetite, many chronic users can become malnourished.

Different means of taking cocaine can produce different adverse effects. Regularly snorting cocaine, for example, can lead to loss of the sense of smell, nosebleeds, problems with swallowing, hoarseness, and a chronically runny nose. Ingesting cocaine can cause severe bowel gangrene due to reduced blood flow. People who inject cocaine can experience severe allergic reactions and, as with all injecting drug users, are at increased risk of contracting HIV and other blood-borne diseases.

Added danger: cocaethylene

When people mix cocaine and alcohol consumption, they are compounding the danger each drug poses and unknowingly forming a complex chemical experiment within their bodies. NIDA-funded researchers have found that the human liver combines cocaine and alcohol and manufactures a third substance, cocaethylene, which intensifies cocaine's euphoric effects, while potentially increasing the risk of sudden death. The risk of an acute heart attack in cocaine abusers is twenty-four times greater if alcohol is also consumed. A 2010 paper published in the European Heart Journal has also indicated that the individuals at risk were usually males in their 20s and 30s and also tobacco smokers. Upwards of 80% of individuals who use performance enhancing drugs, also have experimented with street drugs. Sudden Cardiac Death Syndrome appears to be an increasing or more recognized phenomenon. The etiological cause of death in this large 2010 study was cocaine in over 3% of the victims surveyed. Over 75% of these individuals who had died had also consumed alcohol. This is clearly a lethal combination.

Ecstasy

Ecstasy or MDMA (3,4 methylenedioxymethamphetamine) is a synthetic, psychoactive drug chemically similar to the stimulant methamphetamine and the hallucinogen mescaline. Street names for MDMA include Ecstasy, Adam, XTC, and Love Drug. MDMA is an illegal drug that acts as both a stimulant and psychedelic, producing an energizing effect, as well as distortions in time and perception and enhanced enjoyment from tactile experiences. MDMA exerts its primary effects in the brain on neurons that use the chemical serotonin to communicate with other neurons. The serotonin system plays an important role in regulating mood, aggression, sexual activity, sleep, and sensitivity to pain.

Research in animals indicates that MDMA is neurotoxic; whether or not this is also true in humans is currently an area of intense investigation. MDMA can also be dangerous to health and, on rare occasions, lethal.

Health Hazards

For some people, MDMA can be addictive. A survey of young adult and adolescent MDMA users found that 43% of those who reported ecstasy use met the accepted diagnostic criteria for dependence, as evidenced by continued use despite knowledge of physical or psychological harm, withdrawal effects, and tolerance (or diminished response), and 34% met the criteria for drug abuse. Almost 60% of people who use MDMA report withdrawal symptoms, including fatigue, loss of appetite, depressed feelings, and trouble concentrating.

Cognitive Effects

Chronic users of MDMA perform more poorly than non-users on certain types of cognitive or memory tasks. Some of these effects may be due to the use of other drugs in combination with MDMA, among other factors.

Physical Effects

In high doses, MDMA can interfere with the body's ability to regulate temperature. On rare but unpredictable occasions, this can lead to a sharp increase in body temperature (hyperthermia), resulting in liver, kidney, and cardiovascular system failure, and death.

Because MDMA can interfere with its own metabolism, (breakdown within the body) potentially harmful levels can be reached by repeated drug use within short intervals.

Users of MDMA face many of the same risks as users of other stimulants such as cocaine and amphetamines. These include increases in heart rate and blood pressure, (a special risk for people with circulatory problems or heart disease) and other symptoms such as muscle tension, involuntary teeth clenching, nausea, blurred vision, faintness, and chills or sweating

Psychological Effects
These can include confusion, depression, sleep problems, drug craving, and severe anxiety. These problems can occur during and sometimes days or weeks after taking MDMA.

Neurotoxicity
Research in animals links MDMA exposure to long-term damage to neurons that are involved in mood, thinking, and judgment. A study in non-human primates showed that exposure to MDMA for only four days caused damage to serotonin nerve terminals that was evident six to seven years later. While similar neurotoxicity has not been definitively shown in humans, the wealth of animal research indicating MDMA's damaging properties suggests that MDMA is not a safe drug for human consumption.

Liquid Ecstasy and Sexual Assault
Liquid Ecstasy is a chemical called gama hydroxybutyrate (GHB), and is a different chemical to the compound Ecstasy [MDMA], but it has similar effects. This includes a heightened relaxed state, referred to as a "touchy feely" feeling. This street drug is also commonly used in combination with MDMA. Although it has been claimed that GHB can be potentially used to facilitate sexual assault, no case reports have been previously described. A case is described in which GHB was used with that criminal purpose and a review of previous literature has been undertaken.

An estimated 20% of adult women, 15% of college-aged women and 12% of adolescent girls have experienced sexual assault or sexual abuse. Drug facilitated sexual assault has increasingly occurred in the past few years, and gamma hydroxybutyrate (GHB), best known by the street name of 'liquid ecstasy', has repeatedly been claimed as one of the most commonly used for this purpose. However, objective analytical data demonstrate that GHB is much more unusual than expected and that ethanol is by far the substance more frequently found

Nevertheless, as nothing is reported in these studies about whether drugs were voluntarily consumed by the victim or intentionally used by the perpetrator to gain his/her control, the true role for each drug in sex crimes remains to be defined.

Hidden Risk: Drug Purity

Other drugs chemically similar to MDMA, such as MDA (methylenedioxyamphetamine, the parent drug of MDMA) and PMA (paramethoxyamphetamine) have been associated with fatalities in the U.S. and Australia. These compounds are sometimes sold as ecstasy.

These drugs can be neurotoxic or create additional health risks to the user. Ecstasy tablets may contain other substances in addition to MDMA, such as ephedrine (a stimulant), dextromethorphan (DXM), a cough suppressant, caffeine, cocaine and methamphetamine. While the combination of MDMA with one or more of these drugs may be inherently dangerous, users might also combine them with substances such as marijuana and alcohol, putting themselves at further physical risk.

Extent of Use
National Survey on Drug Use and Health (NSDUH)

In 2004, an estimated 450,000 people in the U.S. aged twelve and older used MDMA in the past thirty days. Ecstasy use dropped significantly among persons aged 18-25 from 14.8% in 2003 to 13.8% in 2004 for lifetime use, and from 3.7 % to 3.1% for past year use. Other 2004 NSDUH results show significant reductions in lifetime and past year use among 18-20 year olds, reductions in past month use for 14-15 year olds, and past year and past month reductions in use among females.

Tobacco and Nicotine

Tobacco smoking is the inhalation of smoke from burnt dried cured leaves of the tobacco plant. The most common form of tobacco smoking is in a cigarette.

People usually smoke tobacco for pleasure. It is considered to be the most satisfactory way of accommodating a nicotine addiction. Tobacco was used by Native Americans back as far as 2000 B.C. The practice was brought to Europe by the explorer Christopher Columbus and his crew. Tobacco smoking was initially sold in Spain. It was introduced to the rest worldwide via trade.

Tobacco is a negative health food product processed from the fresh leaves of plants in the Genus Nicotiana. Tobacco smoke contains nicotine and harmaine which combined gives rise to addictive stimulant and euphoric properties. The effect of nicotine in first time or irregular use is to increase alertness and memory and mild euphoria. Nicotine also disturbs metabolism and suppresses appetite, because nicotine like many stimulants, increases blood sugar levels.

Medical researchers determined that chronic tobacco use can lead to many health problems particularly lung cancer and emphysema. In 1972, the Hill and Doll study also confirmed that tobacco smoking was a significant causative effect of cardiovascular disease.

It is considered that tobacco smoking killed approximately one hundred million people worldwide in the twentieth century and could kill one billion people around the world in the twenty-first century. It is also considered that tobacco smoking results in a death every eight seconds from its use.

Tobacco smoking plays a significant role in many deaths and diseases due to the fact that there are over four thousand chemical compounds present in inhaled smoke, several of which are known carcinogens (cancer-inducing).

In North America, the Surgeon General is appointed to promote health to its citizens. In the 2004 Surgeon General's report on the health consequences of smoking, the conclusions were very stark and very significant namely that smoking causes cancer in parts of the body including the kidney, cervix and bone marrow that have not been previously linked to the smoking in previous reports.

Smoking also diminishes health generally; adverse side effects begin before birth and continue for the life span. Smoking also causes cataracts and contributes to the development of osteoporosis thus increasing the risk of fracture during the later decades of life. Between 1995 and 1999, smoking caused approximately four hundred and forty thousand premature deaths in the United States leading to 13.2 years of potential life loss for male smokers and 14.5 years of lost life for female smokers. Changes in cigarettes that reduce the use of tar and nicotine have not had any significant effect on the general health of the public.

Tobacco smoking is also associated with cancers of the mouth and nasopharynx and throat and many unexplained cancers in these regions are considered to be directly associated with chronic tobacco usage.

Unborn children and children living in houses of people who smoke tobacco are also at significant risk of chronic disease as they grow with adult life.

The major conclusions of the 2004 reports show smoking harms nearly every organ of the body causing many diseases and a reduction in health of smokers in general.

Quitting smoking has immediate as well as long-term benefits in reducing the risk for disease caused by smoking and improving health in general.

The list of diseases caused by smoking has been expanded to include; abdominal aortic aneurysms, acute myeloid leukaemia, cataracts, cervical cancer, kidney cancer, pancreatic cancer, periodontitis and stomach cancers. These are in addition to the diseases previously noted to be caused by smoking such as; bladder, esophageal, laryngeal, lung or throat cancer, chronic lung disease, coronary heart disease, cardiovascular disease as well as reproductive effects and Sudden Infant Death Syndrome.

Modafinil
Modafinil is an approved drug used in the treatment of narcolepsy, shift work sleep disorder, and excessive daytime sleepiness associated with obstructive sleep apnea.

Modafinil, like other stimulants, increases the release of monoamines but also elevates hypothalamic histamine levels, leading some researchers to consider Modafinil a "wakefulness promoting agent" rather than a classic amphetamine-like stimulant.

Modafinil has been shown to be effective in the treatment of Attention-Deficit Hyperactivity Disorder (ADHD), depression, cocaine addiction, Parkinson's Disease, schizophrenia, shift workers' sleep disorder and disease-related fatigue. This drug was detected in a number of athletes' samples in the early 2000's. In the 2003 World Championships, Kelli White, the American sprint sensation, won both the 100 and 200m titles. The stimulant Modafinil was detected in her urine sample. She stated that her doctor prescribed it because she comes from a family of narcolepsy sufferers. This information was not disclosed previously. Modafinil was not on the banned substance list, but was added in to the WADA list in 2003.

Marijuana

Marijuana is a green, brown, or gray mixture of dried, shredded leaves, stems, seeds, and flowers of the hemp plant. You may hear marijuana called by street names such as 'pot', 'herb', 'weed', or 'grass'. All forms of marijuana are mind-altering. In other words, they change how the brain works. They all contain THC (delta-9-tetrahydrocannabinol), the main active chemical in marijuana. They also contain more than four hundred other chemicals. Marijuana's effects on the user depend on its strength or potency, which is related to the amount of THC it contains. The THC content of marijuana has been increasing since the 1970s.

Marijuana is usually smoked as a cigarette (called a joint) or in a pipe or a bong. Recently, it has appeared in cigar wrappers called blunts, when it is often combined with another drug, such as crack cocaine.

THC in marijuana is rapidly absorbed by fatty tissues in various organs. Generally, traces (metabolites) of THC can be detected by standard urine testing methods several days after a smoking session. However, in chronic heavy users, traces can sometimes be detected for weeks after they have stopped using marijuana.

Contrary to popular belief, most teenagers do not use marijuana. Among American students surveyed yearly, between one in four and one in six teenage school children report they are current marijuana users.

The way the drug affects each person depends on many factors, including:

- users previous experience with the drug
- how strong the marijuana is (how much THC it has)
- what the user expects to happen
- where the drug is used
- how it is taken
- whether the user is drinking alcohol or using other drugs

Some people feel nothing at all when they smoke marijuana. Others may feel relaxed or high. Sometimes marijuana makes users feel thirsty and very hungry; an effect commonly referred to as 'the munchies'.

Some users can undergo negative effects from marijuana. They may suffer sudden feelings of anxiety and have paranoid thoughts. This is more likely to happen when a more potent variety of marijuana is used.

The short-term effects of marijuana include
- problems with memory and learning
- distorted perception (sights, sounds, time, touch)
- trouble with thinking and problem solving
- loss of motor coordination
- increased heart rate

These effects are even greater when other drugs are mixed with the marijuana and users do not always know what drugs are given to them.

Marijuana affects memory, judgment and perception. The drug negatively affects your family relationships, school performance and recreational activities. If you're high on marijuana, you are more likely to make mistakes that could embarrass or put you in a compromising situation.

Athletes could find their performance is off; timing, movements, and coordination are all affected by THC. Also, since marijuana can affect judgment and decision making, its use can lead to risky sexual behavior, resulting in exposure to sexually transmitted diseases like HIV, the virus that causes AIDS.

Long-term effects of marijuana use
Research to date shows that regular use of marijuana or THC may play a role in some kinds of cancer and in problems with the respiratory and immune systems.

Cancer
It's hard to know for sure whether regular marijuana use causes cancer, but it is known that marijuana contains some of the same, and sometimes even more, of the cancer-causing chemicals found in tobacco smoke. Studies show that someone who smokes five joints per day may be taking in as many cancer-causing chemicals as someone who smokes a full pack of cigarettes every day.

Lungs and airways
People who smoke marijuana often develop the same kinds of breathing problems that cigarette smokers have: coughing and wheezing. They tend to have more chest colds than non-users. They are also at greater risk of getting lung infections like pneumonia.

Immune system
Animal studies have found that THC can damage the cells and tissues in the body that help protect against disease. When the immune cells are weakened you are more likely to get sick.

Research has also shown that very few young people use other illegal drugs without first trying marijuana; for example, the risk of using cocaine is much greater for those who have tried marijuana than for those who have never tried it. Using marijuana puts children and teens in contact with people who are users and sellers of other drugs. There is a greater risk that a marijuana user will be exposed to and urged to try more drugs. To better determine this risk, scientists are examining the possibility that long-term marijuana use may create changes in the brain that make a person more at risk of becoming addicted to other drugs, such as alcohol or cocaine. Further research is needed to predict who will be at greatest risk.

Some studies show that when people have smoked large amounts of marijuana for years, the drug takes its toll on mental functions. Heavy or daily use of marijuana affects the parts of the brain that control memory, attention, and learning. A working short-term memory is needed to learn and perform tasks that call for more than one or two steps.

Smoking marijuana causes some changes in the brain that are like those caused by cocaine, heroin, and alcohol. Scientists are still learning about the many ways that marijuana can affect the brain.

Long-term marijuana use can lead to addiction in some people. That is, they cannot control their urges to seek out and use marijuana, even though it negatively affects their family relationships, school performance, and recreational activities. According to one study, marijuana use in teenagers who have prior anti-social problems can quickly lead to addiction. With addiction, some frequent, heavy marijuana users develop a tolerance to its effects. This means they need larger and larger amounts of marijuana to get the same desired effects as they used to get from smaller amounts.

Marijuana and Sport

Marijuana is a commonly used street drug and is specifically banned by the National Collegiate Athletic Association (NCAA) in the United States of America. It is banned only for certain Olympic sports such as basketball and boxing; however, many governing sports bodies reserve the right to test athletes for marijuana at competitive events. The active ingredient in marijuana is delta-5-tetrahydro-cannabinol, and metabolites are detectable in the urine four to ten days after smoking a marijuana cigarette. Passive inhalation of marijuana can also cause detectable levels in urine, and the thresholds used by governing bodies should therefore be sufficiently high to take this into account. Marijuana abuse can lead to impaired depth perception, which can be potentially hazardous in high speed or contact sports, where visualization of distance is important.

Methadrone

Methadrone is a popular new street drug sweeping through Great Britain. Not to be confused with methadone, the drug used to wean people off heroin addiction, methadrone is legally sold online or through street dealers. Barley known to the greater population until recently, numerous fatalities where methadrone was a contributing factor has politicians taking notice. Many families of the deceased are demanding Parliament take immediate action to prevent further tragedies.

Methadrone Side-effects

Methadrone, also known as M-C, M-Cat or 'meow meow' is a stimulant with similar characteristics as other amphetamines such as ecstasy. It is usually an off-white powder that is snorted in the same fashion as cocaine. It can also be taken as a bomb, which is methadrone wrapped up in paper and swallowed.

Methadrone is a very harsh drug to ingest. When snorting the substance many users have reported they experience nosebleeds and throat burning sensations. Other side effects include; psychosis, insomnia, cardiac arrest and death. A problem with a methadrone high is that it only lasts a short period of time. Users will binge on the drug to maintain their euphoric experience exposing themselves to greater dangers. Many long-term effects of the drug are not yet known by researchers.

Methadrone is engineered in Chinese laboratories before being shipped into Great Britain. It is mostly sold over the internet for 10-15 pounds sterling a gram. It is listed as not for human consumption online but this is only a strategy used by dealers to avoid prosecution. It is easy to buy over the internet with supply arriving within days of a purchase.

Along with the greater population, many Members of Parliament in Britain were unaware of the drug's existence until late 2009 when an increasing number of fatalities were attributed to methadrone abuse. Parents of deceased children are pleading with Parliament to have the drug be banned and the United Kingdom parliament is working to ban this substance use. The 'legal drug' has become very popular with recreational users and club goers using it in the place of ecstasy and cocaine.

British authorities have pleaded with teenagers to avoid the drug at all costs while Parliament moves in the direction of criminalizing the substance. The drug is already illegal in Denmark, Norway and Sweden. In the past months, both Britain and Ireland have banned the high street sale of the drug by outlawing Head Shops. The drug continues to be sold over the internet.

Chapter 13

DRUG TESTING AND THERAPEUTIC USE EXEMPTION IN COMPETITIVE SPORT

"The Olympic rules and WADA code never contemplated having doped athletes locked up.....Just get them out of sport"
Dick Pound

Performance-enhancing drugs are banned by the majority of sports' governing bodies. The International Olympic Council Medical Commission initially took the lead in defining and classifying banned substances in the 1960's. A performance-enhancing drug user is considered to be one who deliberately uses a drug in an attempt to gain unfair advantage over fellow competitors. In 1986, the IOC produced a list of doping classes and methods. WADA updated the list to the current list in 1999. The World Anti-Doping Agency provides a list every year of banned substances, banned methods, and substances which are banned under certain circumstances. The list is not exhaustive. I include the 2011 list. This is only of relevance to those elite athletes who may be liable to a testing program.

The WADA list is divided into 4 sections:
1. Prohibited substances

2. Prohibited methods

3. Prohibited substances and methods in competition

4. Prohibited substances in certain sports

Prohibited substances
S1. Anabolic Agents
Anabolic agents are prohibited.
1. Anabolic Androgenic Steroids (AAS)
- Exogenous AAS
- Endogenous AAS when administered exogenously
2. Other anabolic agents including but are not limited to: Clenbuterol and selective androgen receptor modulators (SARMs).

S2. Peptide hormones, growth factors and related substances
The following substances and their releasing factors are prohibited:
- Erythropoiesis-Stimulating Agents e.g. erythropoietin (EPO) ans Darbepoetin (Depo)
- Chorionic Gonadotrophin (CG) and Luteinizing Hormone (LH)
- Insulins
- Corticotrophins
- Growth hormone (GH), Insulin-like Growth Factor-1 (IGF-1), Growth Factors (FGFs), Hepatocyte Growth Factor (HGF), Mechano Growth Factors (MGFs), Platelet-Derived Growth Factor (PDGF), Vascular-Endothelial Growth Factor (VEGF) as well as any other growth factor affecting muscle, tendon or ligament protein synthesis/degradation, vascularisation, energy utilization, regenerative capacity or fibre type switching and other substances with similar chemical structure or similar biological effect(s).

S3. Beta 2 Agonists
All beta-2 agonists (including both optical isomers where relevant) are prohibited except salbutamol (maximum 1600 micrograms over twenty-four hours) and salmeterol when taken by inhalation in accordance with manufacturers recommendations.

S4. Hormone antagonists and modulators
The following classes are prohibited:
1. Aromatase inhibitors
2. Selective estrogens receptor modulators (SERMs)
3. Other anti-estrogenic substances
4. Agents modifying myostatin function

S5. Diuretics and other masking agents
Masking agents are prohibited. They include: diuretics, probenecid and other substances with similar biological effects in masking effects.

Prohibited Methods
M1. Enhancement of Oxygen Transfer
The following are prohibited:

- Blood doping, including the use of autologous, homologous or heterologous blood or red blood cell products of any origin.

- Artificially enhancing the uptake, transport or delivery of oxygen

M2. Chemical and Physical Manipulation
The following is prohibited:
1. Tampering, or attempting to tamper, in order to alter the integrity and validity of Samples collected during Doping Control is prohibited.

2. Intravenous infusions are prohibited except for those legitimately received in the course of hospital admissions or clinical investigations.

3. Sequential withdrawal, manipulation and reinfusion of whole blood into the circulatory system is prohibited.

M3. Gene Doping
The following, with the potential to enhance sport performance, are prohibited:

1. The transfer of nucleic acids or nucleic acid sequences
2. The use of normal or genetically modified cells
3. The use of agents that directly or indirectly affect functions known to influence performance by altering gene expression

Substances and Methods Prohibited In-Competition
In addition to the categories S0 to S5 and M1 to M3 defined above, the following categories are prohibited during In-Competition

Prohibited Substances
S6. Stimulants:
All stimulants are prohibited, except imidazole derivatives for topical use.
Adrenaline associated with local anaesthetic agents or by local administration (e.g. nasal, ophthalmologic) is not prohibited.
Ephedrine and methyl ephedrine is prohibited when its concentration in urine is greater than ten micrograms per millilitre. Pseudoephedrine is prohibited when its concentration in urine is greater than one hundred and fifty micrograms per millilitre.

S7. Narcotics

S8. Cannabinoids

S9. Glucocoritcosteroids
All glucocorticosteroids are prohibited when administered by oral, intravenous, intramuscular or rectal routes.

Substances prohibited in particular sports
P1. Alcohol
Alcohol (ethanol) is prohibited in competition only, in the sports listed below. Detection will be conducted by analysis of breath and/or blood. The doping violation threshold (haematological values) is 0.10 g/L.

- Aeronautic (FAI)
- Archery (FITA)
- Automobile (FIA)
- Karate (WKF)
- Motorcycling (FIM)
- Ninepin and Tenpin Bowling (FIQ)
- Power-boating (UIM)

P2. Beta-Blockers
Unless otherwise specified, beta-blockers are prohibited during In-Competition only, in the following sports.

- Aeronautic (FAI)
- Archery (FITA) (also prohibited out of competition)
- Automobile (FIA)
- Billiards and Snooker (WCBS)
- Bobsleigh and Skeleton (FIBT)
- Boules (CMSB)
- Bridge (FMB)
- Curling (WCF)
- Darts (WDF)
- Golf (IGF)
- Motorcycling (FIM)
- Modern Pentathlon (UIPM) for disciplines involving shooting
- Ninepin and Tenpin Bowling (FIQ)
- Power-boating (UIM)
- Sailing (ISAF) for match race helms only
- Shooting (ISSF, IPC) (also prohibited out of competition)

- Skiing/Snowboarding (FIS) in ski-jumping, freestyle aerials/ halfpipe and snowboard halfpipe/big air
- Wrestling (FILA)

This list of drugs is not comprehensive, and includes the addendum that related compounds are also banned.

It is important that physicians involved in sports medicine are aware of the up-to-date listing of doping classes and methods relating to particular sports as these vary from one sport to another. Drug testing commenced in 1967 at the Grenoble Olympic Games.

Drug testing, however, is not a feature of all recreational or competitive sports, but rather a reserve for elite sportsmen and sportswomen.

The World Anti-Doping Agency (WADA) bans substances if they meet two of the following three criteria:

1. The agent is performance enhancing
2. The agent is potentially dangerous
3. The agent is against the ethos of sport

Anti-doping rules are in place to make sport safe for the participant and as a byproduct to make sport fairer. Athletes like all humans get sick. Athletes need to be treated correctly, and athletes are also people requiring appropriate confidentiality, and understanding should they run into medical problems.

Up to recently many athletes avoided taking prescribed medication for fear of breaking the doping rules of sport. One of the corner stones of the anti-doping policy is to ensure that sports participation is safe and health-promoting, not the opposite. With the advent of WADA, provision was made to accommodate athletes who had a genuine need to take medication, which in other circumstances would be considered to be performance-enhancing. This was referred to as a Therapeutic Use Exemption or TUE.

Therapeutic Use Exemption is a method whereby a sick athlete can receive appropriate medical care without compromising his athletic performance or sporting career.

Information is readily available to all doctors about what substances are allowed; and which ones are banned in sport. Doctors drug reference compendiums all now have information and color coding to assist the medical practitioner in treating elite athletes.

Who is liable to be tested and who needs a TUE?

In all anti-doping programs there are Registered Testing Pools. These are the pools of top level athletes established separately by each international federation and Sports Council. In the case of the Irish Sports Council they will subject athletes in its Registered Testing Pools to both In-Competition and Out-of-Competition Testing.

Athletes designated by one or more international federations as being within the Registered Testing Pool of the International Federation are called 'International-Level Athletes'. In Ireland athletes, other than International-level Athletes, who are designated by the Irish Sports Council as being within the Irish Sports Council Registered Testing Pool are called 'National-Level Athletes'.

Therapeutic Use Exemptions (TUE)

New rules and evolving patterns of abuse and abusers will require greater use of TUEs to identify and treat bona fide cases. TUEs ensure that the ill are treated appropriately, and the doctor is not prevented from delivering best practice to his patient. The system also ensures that the abuser cannot find refuge in a bogus medical case.

Where an athlete needs to use a prohibited substance or method because of a medical condition from which they suffer, they must obtain a Therapeutic Use Exemption, known as a TUE, from the National Sports Council or the international federation of the national governing body concerned. The athlete must have been granted this TUE prior to his or her participation in any sports event.

The increasing numbers of asthmatics, diabetics and individuals with hormonal disorders, and indeed those elite athletes with potentially fatal medical diagnoses such as cancer and narcolepsy, it is a cause of great concern among the medical and sporting communities. These diagnoses confer the right to use potentially performance-enhancing drugs. While the majority of doctors and athletes are above reproach, the rules as they existed allowed room for manoeuvre for a potential abuser. The abuser would use a 'constructed' medical diagnosis to fraudulently obtain a TUE allowing him or her to use a performance enhancing agent. Sadly there are a small but active group of rogue practitioner's who assist the abusing athlete. Therefore very strict rules and regulations exist to obtain a TUE. The bar had to be raised to avoid this potential pit fall.

Abusing medication in an uncontrolled setting can have disastrous consequences. For example taking asthma medication when you do not have this condition can be as dangerous as not taking appropriate medication for this serious condition. Beta 2 agonists such as Salbutamol are used to treat this condition. These drugs can have a toxic effect on the myocardium and are significantly associated with cardiac arrhythmias. Excessive or inappropriate use of these agents may result in potentially fatal cardiac rhythms, which may manifest themselves during the stress of exercise. The medical welfare of the athlete is a primary concern and as a result all prohibited substances and those which are subject to certain restrictions must be reported by the prescribing doctor to the relevant governing body and a TUE medical committee will confirm permission to use the relevant agent. This protects the athlete, his/her doctor and the integrity of the sport.

There are two methods of gaining a TUE:
1. Standard process
2. Abbreviated process

Both have a separate application form and methodology for gaining the Therapeutic Use Exemption.

Standard Process
1. The TUE will only be considered following the receipt of a completed standard application form.

2. An athlete may not apply to more than one Anti-Doping Organisations for a TUE.

3. The applicant must list any previous and/or current requests, the body to whom that request was made and the decision of that body. A comprehensive medical history, the results of all examinations, laboratory investigations and imaging studies relevant to the applicant must be included. They must list any previous and/or current requests for permission to use a prohibited substance or method, the body to whom the request was made and their decision. They many include a statement by an appropriately trained and qualified physician attesting to the necessity of the otherwise prohibited Substance or Prohibited Method. They must list the dose, frequency, route and duration of administration.

4. Any additional investigations, examinations or imaging studies requested by the TUEC will be undertaken at the expense of the applicant.

5. The decision of the TUEC will be conveyed in writing by the National Sports Council to the athlete, and if applicable

to the athlete's National Governing Body (NGB) and World Anti-Doping Agency. Information will include the duration of the exemption and any associated conditions. An example of how the process operates is outlined as follows: A renal failure patient who has had a kidney transplant applies for permission to use Erythropoietin for the treatment of the chronic anaemia, which accompanies their condition. The patient and his doctors submit an application form to his or her NGB seeking a TUE for the use of this banned substance for the normal treatment of this medical condition. The application will be accompanied by relevant medical documentation relating to the medical condition (such as blood and urinary chemistry) and confirmation of the renal transplantation from the surgeon. This file is reviewed by the TUE chairman and committee, and should the file be in order the athlete will be informed of the granting of TUE. Should this athlete be the subject of a drug test any positive findings relating to Erythropoietin will not result in any action as long as the TUE is in place.

Abbreviated Process

Some prohibited substances are frequently used to treat medical conditions that are frequently encountered in the athlete population. In circumstances such as this a full application is not necessary. Instead the athlete can avail of the abbreviated Therapeutic Use Exemption Application process.

This abbreviated application process is strictly limited to beta-2 agonists (formoterol, salbutanmol, salmetaterol and terbutaline) by inhalation and glucocorticosteroids by non-systemic routes.

Should an athlete wish to use one of these substances a medical notification justifying the necessity to use the substance must be submitted to the National Sports Council.

The notification should be in the approved format and once the Irish Sports Council receives a complete notification the applicant will be granted approval for use of the prohibited substance. However, if the notification is incomplete the application shall be returned to the athlete concerned.

The rules provide that International Level Athletes and athletes competing in international events apply for a TUE from the international federation concerned. National-Level Athletes and athletes competing in Irish national events apply for a TUE from the Irish Sports Council.

There is an onus upon athletes who have been granted a TUE from their International Federation to report that granting to the Irish Sports Council and the NGB concerned immediately, and to furnish the Irish Sports Council and the NGB concerned with all relevant information and documentation.

TUE Committee
A TUE Committee of no less than three doctors is appointed by the National Sports Council. The purpose of this committee is to consider requests for TUE. Where a TUE request is received by the Sports Council, the chair of the TUEC will appoint one or more members of the committee to consider the request. The committee member(s) will evaluate the request promptly and in accordance with the International Standard for Therapeutic Use Exemptions. The administration and determination of such an application will be conducted confidentially necessary and the TUEC may seek additional medical information from the athlete concerned. The responsibility for complying with this request rests fully on the athlete.

Criteria in granting a TUE
There are certain criteria by which an application for a TUE is judged. These are as follows:

Whether or not the athlete would suffer a significant impairment to his/her health if the prohibited substance or methods were to be withheld, in the course of treating an acute or chronic medical condition. No additional enhancement of performance should be created by the therapeutic use of the prohibited substance or method other than that which might be anticipated by the return to a state of normal health following the treatment of a legitimate medical condition.

There is no reasonable therapeutic alternative which could be used instead of the prohibited substance or method; the need to use the prohibited substance or method must not be due to the athlete having previously used a prohibited substance or method in a non-therapeutic manner.

A completed application form in the approved format must be submitted in order for the TUE application to be considered. If the TUEC feels it necessary to conduct additional relevant investigations, examinations or imaging studies these should be undertaken at the expense of the athlete or alternatively at the expense of his or her NGB. No liability will arise for any inconvenience or loss caused.

Conclusion

The TUE process is fair and assists athletes to compete in a controlled environment. It also ensures that an athlete with a real medical condition will not be inconvenienced by his condition; and allowed participate in sport without any impairment to his health and performance. Doctors are well aware of the rules and methods of TUE. In the initial years of the WADA rules mistakes were made by athletes failing to complete paper work. If the paperwork is in order almost all athletes with any medical conditions can compete safely and within the rules of sport.

It is essential, however, that all medicines or potential medicines are prescribed by a medical practitioner following an appropriate medical consultation examination and possible test. Taking a medicine such as an inhaler, because a fellow team-mate was using an asthma medication, was common practice in the 1980s and 1990s. This is inappropriate and will result in a drug infraction.

The role of the doctor cannot be over emphasized. At an international event some years ago, an athlete under my care was prescribed a cold remedy by her running coach. The product was one of nine that a particular North American Pharmaceutical company produced. Six of the products did not contain the then banned substance ephedrine.

The coach, a non medic prescribed one of the three agents which contained the banned substance. After her run in the heats the athlete's name was drawn out for a drug test. To her amazement she tested positive and suffered the humiliation and embarrassment of a positive drug test and sanction. All of this occurred unwittingly. Had she simply consulted a medical practitioner all would have been avoided. The story underscores the need for diligence when taking medicines; no one in this example wishes to take a performance-enhancing drug, gain an edge or break the rules. Zero tolerance and strict liability is the level of proof associated with drug testing. So despite the fact an honest mistake had occurred no leniency was available, and the athlete had to suffer the sanction imposed on her by the anti-doping authorities, for a mistake made by her coach. Had the drug been necessary the doctor would have applied for a TUE, or more likely selected another medication which was allowable.

Chapter 14

LEGAL PERFORMANCE ENHANCEMENT

"Regimen is superior to medicine"
Voltaire

The preceding chapters have gone through in detail the type of motivation that causes a young athlete to get involved in performance-enhancing drug abuse. These chapters also clearly outline the history of the abuse of substances and significantly how morbidity and occasional mortality can visit those individuals who tamper with performance-enhancing agents.

Telling young people what not to do is often a flawed method of getting your message over. In many instances a positive message about how to achieve their desired end point or goal may yield a much higher uptake by young athletes. Therefore if an athlete or young person wishes to enhance his performance or improve his bodily function and ability to train hard and achieve both muscular and physiological endurance function then these endeavours should be encouraged and assisted. He should be guided to other methods of gaining this performance enhancement.

Sports science and sports medicine have clearly outlined four specific areas where appropriate attention to detail can yield great results in the area of performance enhancement, they are: **hydration, alcohol avoidance, appropriate nutrition and sleep.**

Hydration
Dehydration or poor hydration is by far the single biggest failing of the modern athlete and exerciser. Research has clearly shown that an adequately hydrated individual will perform his sport or activity at a competent or a super competent level. Any element of dehydration has a significant effect on physiological

function and in particular on aerobic function. Dehydration of 2% of the body weight is associated with significant reduction in aerobic function of the order of 8-10%.

Dehydration is easy to measure in the training athlete. Hydration can be simply measured by body weight. One pound of body weight is equal to one pint of fluid, though this usually only works well in the elite or fit young athletes who are at a stable base. Those individuals who are overweight may lose body fat rather than fluid.

If a fit individual with a normal and stable body weight of two hundred pounds who trains regularly looses four pounds in an exercise session or finds himself to be four pounds lighter before an exercise session, then it can be assumed that he is four pints behind in fluid. He should immediately make up this difference.

In the equestrian world, no race horse has ever been allowed out on the gallops unless his urine is crystal clear. In this way, the veterinary surgeons and horse trainers assess hydration. If your urine is anything other than crystal clear, then you are probably dehydrated. Yellow or dark coloured urine implies significant dehydration and taking exercise in these circumstances will undoubtedly result in a poor athletic performance.

This also goes for more moderate intensity pursuits such as lighter tennis, bicycle riding and golf. It is a good habit to assess your hydration on a daily basis and to ensure that you are adequately hydrated. Most top class athletes will ensure that they drink three to four litres of water every day. It is not necessary to drink any special isotonic or 'special' fluid. If your body is used to taking in water, then this will adequately hydrate you. The best course of action is to start slowly with two to two and a half litres of fluids a day and try and build this up to three to four litres a day. Properly hydrated athletes will perform better. Failing to be dehydrated will result in a deficiency of up to 8% and this has to be avoided.

Alcohol

Alcohol is probably the greatest bug bear of the athletic population. Researchers indicated in North America that 88% of top class athletes drink alcohol regularly. In Ireland, this number is over 90%. Alcohol is not the friend of the athlete. Research at Trinity College Dublin, has shown that the hangover effect of alcohol has a significantly deleterious effect on aerobic performance. The aerobic function is reduced by an average of 11.4% in the hangover phase (twelve hours after consuming alcohol).

The actual amount of alcohol consumed has a variable effect on physiological function. Even small amounts of alcohol may result in a significant reduction in aerobic function and there is an enormous person to person variability. If you are sensitive to alcohol or have a slow metabolism, you may in fact suffer from the hangover effect of alcohol for many days after drinking a small quantity of alcohol. The reason for the hangover effect of alcohol is three fold:

1. The effect alcohol has on the production of aerobic energy
2. The dehydrating effect of alcohol
3. The psychological effect of alcohol

Aerobic energy is produced by the breaking down of carbohydrate through the Embden-Meyerhof pathway, the citric acid cycle and on to the electron transport chain where energy for muscle contraction is made.

CARBOHYDRATE

E.M.P.

C.A.C.

E.T.C.   **ENERGY**

If you drink alcohol, the alcohol is metabolised in the liver by an enzyme called alcohol dehydrogenase. The reaction uses a chemical substrate called NAD. The byproduct of this reaction is a second substrate called NADH. As alcohol is metabolysied large quantities of NADH accumulate. These larger quantities of NADH which accumulate following alcohol metabolism can affect aerobic metabolism by diverting carbohydrate metabolism away from Pyruvate Acid production, and towards Lactic Acid production. Large amounts of acids are produced in the metabolism of alcohol. During the normal course of event, the buffering system in our bodies mop off this acid. If however, one then engages in athletic performance, further amounts of acid are produced and the buffering system reaches capacity because so much has been used in mopping up the alcohol metabolites. Therefore the following day, when one is taking exercise, early fatigue is developed because there are higher levels of acid accumulation in the blood which are not offered in the normal way.

This also has a knock-on effect in the citric acid cycle where further metabolism of sugar is performed at the mallate-oxaloacetate step in the citric acid cycle; there is significant slowing in metabolism again caused by the elevation in NADH. This has a knock-on effect in the generation of energy in the electron transport chain and thus there is less energy produced as the energy systems have been taken off by dealing with the metabolism of alcohol. This too has a significant knock-on effect on aerobic performance.

Alcohol is a significant diuretic and the following day after imbibing alcohol, dehydration is also a common consequence. As outlined, dehydration of 2% of the body weight will have a significant effect on overall aerobic function of the order of 8%. The psychological effect of imbibing alcohol should not be underestimated. If one has consumed alcohol the night before, one may have a hangover or generally feel unwell or psychologically not up for a proper engagement in one's sporting activity. This psychological component has also been frequently seen in those who become injured in the second half of sporting events as fatigue and lack of energy results in inappropriate decisions and choices on the sporting field.

Avoidance, therefore, of alcohol is another significant way of improving your aerobic function. If an athlete on a football team trains hard for 6 months he will do well to improve his aerobic function by 8 or 10%. If however, the night before he performs, he drank a number of bottles of beer, this fitness gain would be lost by one simple act. Therefore avoiding alcohol would provide a significant athletic gain.

Nutrition

There is an enormous industry built up over the last twenty-five years in the production of sports supplements and special foods. It should never be forgotten that a normal balanced diet will provide sufficient nutrition, minerals, and vitamins for any exercising athlete. There is never a need to take extra vitamin supplements or minerals if the athlete has an adequate diet. This can be clearly seen in the case of iron tablets. 92% of female athletes in North America take iron supplements. This is unnecessary in almost all cases.

No research has ever shown that iron supplementation (in an individual who has normal iron stores) will have an improvement in aerobic or athletic function. This is simply because the body can only handle a certain amount of iron. 100 mcg a day is all the body is capable of storing and requiring. If an individual takes in excessive amounts of iron, then simply the iron will be excreted. The problem with iron is that it is tantamount to pouring water into a glass that is already full. The iron simply spills out of the glass and is excreted into the urine. Many individuals believe that they are doing no harm by taking in substances such as iron but iron supplementation also comes with significant side effects. Constipation, headaches, rashes are all associated with the excessive use of iron including gastrointestinal disturbances.

If iron is injected in a normochromic [non anemic] individual, (normal iron levels) then no exercise advantage will be gained but you are courting the possibility of a one in a hundred anaphylactic reaction (allergic shock). While these side effects appear to be quite rare, it is an unnecessary risk to take considering there is no benefit in taking the substance in the first instance. Similar examples could be given with Folic acid, vitamin A, vitamin B, vitamin C and vitamin D. These agents are frequently taken by the exercising athlete with no particular advantage and no particular reason to imbibe the substances, with an ever present risk of a side effect.

If an athlete in daily training consumes a normal balanced diet of 55% carbohydrate, 20% protein and 25% fat of over 3500 to 4000 calories a day, he will undoubtedly achieve the normal daily recommended allowances for all the vitamins, and minerals and the major nutritional classes (namely carbohydrate, protein and fat). The use of protein shakes and similar products are simply loading the body with a substance that may be hard to metabolise and handle. Simply taking in substances such as eggs and meat will more than adequately supply your body with the protein requirements for normal exercise. Therefore a normal balanced diet with adequate calorie intake will ensure that your performance will not be in any way altered by your nutritional status.

In short, these 3 simple areas, if they are attended to and approached in a systematic fashion, will give you a significant performance enhancement. If the exercising athlete attempts to avoid alcohol, becomes adequately hydrated and tries to achieve a mixed diet of between 3500 and 4000 calories an enhanced performance will undoubtedly be assured.

Sleep

Sleep is also a component which should never be overlooked. Many exercising athletes do not have adequate sleep. Research has indicated that a minimum of six to seven hours of sleep at night is required for the exercising athlete. One's sleeping pattern should also ensure that one goes to bed at a similar time every night and that, hours before midnight, are probably the most beneficial hours for the exercising athlete.

Research from 2007 has shown that extra sleep will improve athletes' performances. Athletes who get an extra amount of sleep are more likely to improve their performance in a game. Recent research at Stanford University conducted a study on a group of healthy students on the Stanford men's basketball team, who maintained their typical sleep-wake patterns for a two-week baseline followed by an extended sleep period in which they obtained as much extra sleep as possible. To assess improvements in athletic performance, the students were judged based on their sprint time and shooting percentages. Significant improvements in athletic performance were observed, including faster sprint time and increased free-throws. Athletes also reported increased energy and improved mood during practices and games, as well as a decreased level of fatigue.

Subsequent research by the same author from 2008 has shown both physical and psychological benefit from extra sleep in a group of collegiate swimmers.

The swimmers gained an additional competitive edge to perform at their highest level. This study agrees with data from other studies of different sports and suggests that athletes across all sports can improve their athletic performance by decreasing their weekly accumulated sleep debt.

The study showed that daytime sleepiness decreased significantly with extra sleep, while mood improvements related to getting extra sleep included higher ratings of vigour and lower ratings of fatigue. Many athletes accumulate a large sleep debt by not obtaining their individual sleep requirement each night. This can have detrimental effects on cognitive function, mood, and reaction time. These negative effects can be minimized or eliminated by prioritizing sleep in general and, more specifically, obtaining extra sleep to reduce one's sleep debt.

These four remedies would appear to be a simple, and a puritanical approach to performance enhancement, however, the research is clear and the data conclusive. These four areas will ensure an enhancement of performance. Taking all four together, it is likely that you would improve your overall athletic performance in the order of 13-14% which is almost double what any athletic coach would expect. Therefore, while not glamorous, if these areas are addressed carefully and applied to your weekly routine, your training may yield significant dividends, and your performance enhanced safely and successfully.

Chapter 15

Your role and responsibility with a performance enhancing drug abuser

"If you want children to keep their feet on the ground, put some responsibility on their shoulders".
Abigail Van Buren

Parents, Teachers and Guardians; what is your role and responsibility with a performance enhancing drug abuser?

Drug abuse and misuse in Sport is a real and present entity. As parents, guardians and teachers become more aware of this potential in their immediate sphere of influence; action is often taken in a knee jerk fashion. This may drive the abuse underground, where you will be unable to impact on an abuser.

A thoughtful approach is needed. As with any child, telling them not to do something, "because I say so" often has the directly opposite effect. Telling them to stop because the agents will make them sick in the long run also falls on deaf ears, because "the expert" at the gym or club or school ground, has a much more compelling story laced with tales of sporting success, social successes with the opposite sex and total safety in use. A parent, who is seen to be out of touch, can never counter the fool proof mantra of the performance enhancing drug peddler.

A reasoned careful approach in dealing with a young performance enhancing drug abuser is essential for a successful interception of their action and mind set.

Addiction is a complex disorder characterized by compulsive drug use. People who are addicted feel an overwhelming, uncontrollable need for a drug, even in the face of clear negative consequences of the use of such substances. This self-destructive behavior can be hard to understand. Why continue doing something that's hurting you? Why is it so hard to stop? The answer lies in the brain. Repeated street drug abuse alters the brain—causing long-lasting changes to the way it looks and functions. These brain changes interfere with your ability to think clearly, exercise good judgment, control your behaviour, and feel normal without drugs.

These changes are also responsible, in a large part, for the drug cravings and compulsion to use that make addiction so powerful.

In the case of performance enhancing drug abuse the craving and compulsion may not all be a physiological need for the drug, but a craving and compulsion for the effects of the performance enhancing drugs: stronger, leaner and a perception of greater attractiveness.

The path to all drug addiction starts with experimentation. Over 11% of schoolboys and 3% of school girls in North America have experimented with performance enhancing drugs. Young people may try drugs out of curiosity, because friends are doing it, or in an effort to erase another problem; feelings of weakness, unattractiveness or a desire to change physically. At first, the substance seems to solve the problem or make life better, so they use the drug more and more. This is probably the best opportunity to change the pattern of behaviour.

But as the addiction progresses, getting and using the drug becomes more and more important and the ability to stop using is compromised. Stopping may mean getting physically smaller, or putting body fat back on, and turning ones back on the positive comments people have made about your physical appearance since you started abusing performance enhancing agents. What begins as a voluntary choice turns into a physical and psychological need. The good news is that performance enhancing drug addiction is treatable. With treatment and support, you can counteract the disruptive effects of addiction and regain control of your life.

Education is the cornerstone in preventing society as a whole condoning or ignoring this pattern of activity. Little information is available to parents and guardians. Young people often become informed through individuals who have a vested interest in them becoming an abuser, for reasons of peer and herd dynamics, or for financial reasons. Your child may be seen as another potentially happy and ultimately unhappy customer to the drug peddler.

In North America great advances in the area have been made by educating young people to the "pros and cons" of this form of drug abuse. It appears that morality and moral reasoning are still strong in the pre 14 year old child.

Teaching a class which informs in a non judgmental way puts the case simply, and often a young person will make his/her own informed decision as to their participation in this activity. Is it now time to teach this subject formally in our schools?

If you suspect that a son, daughter or school pupil has a drug problem, here are a few things you can do:

Confront

Talk to the person about your concerns, and offer your help and support. The earlier addiction is treated, the better. Don't wait for your loved one to hit rock bottom! Be prepared for excuses and denial of specific examples of behaviour that have you worried. In the first instance listen and try and avoid being judgemental. You will not solve the problem in one fell swoop. Identifying a problem and confronting the issues is only a start

Protect yourself

Don't get so caught up in someone else's drug problem with the effect that you neglect your own needs. Make sure you the parent or guardian have people you can talk to and lean on for support. And stay safe. Don't put yourself in dangerous situations, by confronting suppliers or entering into the murky world of drug trafficking and supply. This is unnecessary and will not impact on your child's behaviour. In many cases a parent will blame themselves for a child's behaviour. This is both unnecessary and unhelpful.

Don't cover for the drug user

Don't make excuses or try to hide the problem. It's natural to want to help a loved one in need, but protecting them from the negative consequences of their choices may keep them from getting the help they need.

Avoid self-blame

You can support a person with a performance enhancing drug abuse problem and encourage treatment, but you can't force an addict to change. You can't control your loved one's decisions. Let the person accept responsibility for his or her actions, an essential step along the way to recovery for addiction.

Professional help

Performance enhancing drug abuse is like any other form of drug abuse. Support is essential to addiction recovery. This can come from family members or close friends. However, professional help is usually required in cases where the young person continues to abuse substances.

According to several studies, drug treatment reduces drug use by 40 to 60 percent and significantly decreases criminal activity during and after treatment. Treatment can improve the prospects for employment. Many performance enhancing abusers spend their waking hours in the gym, thus avoiding normal work or study. Gains of up to 40 percent of work employment after treatment have been reported.

Addiction is a complex but treatable condition. It is characterized by compulsive drug craving, seeking, and use that persist even in the face of severe adverse consequences. Through treatment tailored to individual needs, people with drug addiction can recover and lead fulfilling lives. The ultimate goal of addiction treatment is to enable an individual to achieve lasting abstinence, but the immediate goals are to reduce substance abuse, improve the patient's ability to function, and minimize the medical and social complications of the performance enhancing substance abuse.

In many instances a number of consultations with your GP may be sufficient to halt the abuser. Blood test and medical investigations often identify the damage that is being done to major organs, such as the liver and heart. The realization of the consequences of their actions is often enough for the young person to change their pattern of behavior and cease the abusive activity. In more resistant cases further referral to a psychiatric unit with resources such as councilors, psychologists and therapists may be required. In these instances the performance enhancing drug abuse is dealt with in a similar manner to other drug addictions.

Disseminate and Educate
If a young person is abusing a performance enhancing substance or any substance, it is unlikely that they are not doing it alone. Should an abuser or group be identified then this should be a signal to the school, club or a parents' association to set up an educational forum to advise others in the circle of influence of the potential side effect of this pattern of activity. This forum should be a non judgemental, simple effort to educate the young people on the effect and possible side effects of performance enhancing drug use.

The doctor's role

In the past 10 years the British Medical Council and the World Medical Association have released statements regarding doctors' responsibility and professional conduct in relation to doping in sport. It is unethical for a doctor to provide drugs or treatment for doping. Sports doctors are involved in both the treatment and performance improvement of their charges. These doctors also have a role in monitoring the actions of their patients, always remembering that their ethical responsibility is to the patient, rather than to society in general. This is often a difficult tight rope to walk. A doctor may be consulted for advice regarding the side effects of performance enhancing agents, or he may be faced with an individual who endeavors to 'dupe' the doctor into prescribing medicines which may contravene the regulations and rules of sport.

The health and well being of the patient is paramount, and therefore the doctor has to adopt a pragmatic approach in advising individuals about the risks and dangers of certain drugs, and how these risks could be minimalised, if the individual cannot be convinced to cease his drug abuse. In a similar way, many hospitals provide needle exchange programs which are frequently used by Anabolic steroid abusers to ensure that if this activity takes place it does so in a relatively risk free environment where needle transmitted disease spread can be minimalised. Your doctor is there to help you, not judge you.

Over the past two decades courses and resources regarding medical education in the area of performance enhancing drug abuse have become available to doctors. Throughout the UK and Ireland post-graduate programmes and courses exist to update practicing doctors. Therefore if your son, daughter or loved one is contemplating or is using performance enhancing agents your family doctor should be the first resource you contact.

AFTERWORD

All that glitters is not gold
Often have you hear that told
Many a man his life has sold
William Shakespeare. The Merchant of Venice.

On the 17th of January 2013 Lance Armstrong , the 7 times Tour De France champion admitted a life time of performance enhancing drug abuse. He received a life time ban from competitive sports, and was stripped of his 7 Tour De France titles. He has been asked to return his Olympic bronze medal. His admission came on foot of his exposure by the United States Anti-Doping Agency(USADA), when many of his former team members testified against him. He admitted to using Erythropoietin, Growth Hormone and Anabolic Steroids. The latter 2 substances are associated with a cancer risk. Armstrong suffered from testicular cancer during his cycling career. Steroids are also associated with inappropriate psychological feelings and behaviours. His story contains references to his feelings of invincibility, and single minded aggression to achieve certain goals, with significant consequences to those who opposed him. His fall from grace, like many others before him, is punctuated with references to "passing drug tests" and sham science.

On a personal level, it yet another sporting tragedy played out in the glow of the media light, with spin doctors at every corner altering the glare. On a wider level the Armstrong story helps to underscore the need for us all, to take responsibility ourselves, for the pervasive problem of drugs in sport and in the wider society. We should critically question this behaviour pattern, rather than depend on the rules of sport to define and dictate our own morality.

Drug abuse, be it in sport or society at large is wrong. It carries many obvious as well as hidden risks. Many young people innocently start off on this road, in the hope of attaining